LIFE OF THE HUMAN SOUL

and its Relation to World Evolution

LIFE OF THE HUMAN SOUL

and its Relation to World Evolution

Nine lectures given in Dornach between 29 April and 17 June 1922

TRANSLATED BY MATTHEW BARTON

INTRODUCTION BY MATTHEW BARTON

RUDOLF STEINER

RUDOLF STEINER PRESS

CW 212

The publishers gratefully acknowledge the generous funding of this publication by the estate of Dr Eva Frommer MD (1927–2004) and the Anthroposophical Society in Great Britain

Rudolf Steiner Press
Hillside House, The Square
Forest Row, RH18 5ES

www.rudolfsteinerpress.com

Published by Rudolf Steiner Press 2016

Originally published in German under the title *Menschliches Seelenleben und Geistesstreben im Zusammenhange mit Welt- und Erdentwickelung* (volume 212 in the *Rudolf Steiner Gesamtausgabe* or Collected Works) by Rudolf Steiner Verlag, Dornach. Based on shorthand notes that were not reviewed or revised by the speaker. This authorized translation is based on latest available (second) edition (1998), edited by Hendrik Knobel

Published by permission of the Rudolf Steiner Nachlassverwaltung, Dornach

A catalogue record for this book is available from the British Library

ISBN 978 1 85584 529 9

Cover by Mary Giddens
Typeset by DP Photosetting, Neath, West Glamorgan
Printed and bound by 4edge Limited, UK

CONTENTS

EDITOR'S PREFACE

In the first few months of 1922, Rudolf Steiner undertook a series of lecture tours in various countries. On two of these, organized by the concert agency Wolff & Sachs in various German cities, he gave public lectures on 'The Nature of Anthroposophy' and 'Anthroposophy and Spirit Knowledge', lectured at School of Spiritual Science courses in Berlin and The Hague, and spoke in London as part of the 'New Ideals in Education' events. Between these trips he returned to Dornach for a few days, and gave lectures to members there. The lectures in the present volume belong to those, and were given over three weekends in Dornach.

INTRODUCTION

How are we connected to the world around us? This question, says Steiner, is one that lives subliminally in us, drawing us into deep realms of the psyche where, mostly, our little candle of consciousness flickers and goes out. Spiritual schooling can light it again, so that we learn to perceive and fathom realms of our being beyond the circumscribed and isolated self. In such enquiries, Steiner takes us by the hand, as it were, and reveals a hugely complex picture of interrelationship that cannot be summed up in easy tenets or intellectual principles, because we here meet the sway and surge of life itself. Following him—by reading this book for instance—feels like wrestling continually with our own fixed ideas and perceptions. We are not *one* thing but a unity of multiple qualities invested in the world in many different ways. Our head, heart, lungs and limbs, for instance, all reveal subtly different qualities of connection with both visible and invisible realities that sustain us. Apart from spiritual investigators, perhaps only poets sometimes manage to approach, intuitively, some of the insights which Steiner spells out so lucidly here. When he says, for instance, that our eyes only gradually evolved into organs of sight and were once vital organs as our lungs are now, and that the latter will evolve similarly to grant us another but different form of perception, we might think of a wonderful poem by Rilke—one of his *Sonnets to Orpheus*—that seems to comprehend something of this seemingly strange idea, and of the ineffable, active connection between ourselves and the cosmos.

> Breathing, you invisible poem!
> Continually you trade
> pure space for my own being. Counterweight
> in which I live as rhythm.

Single wave whose gradual
sea I am;
you thriftiest of all oceans—swell
of ever-growing room.

How many of those realms of space were once
within me? Sometimes it seems a breeze
might be my son.

Do you know me still, air,
full of places once mine?
You who were once the pure
leaf of my words, their budding and rind.

Like the poet, Steiner is hard to understand. But we can sense something vivid, alive and profound in his thoughts: we have to deepen and broaden to grasp him, have to become more imaginative and intuitive to keep up with him. It is impossible here to summarize the range and complexity of his ideas, but let's just take another pithy comment: that ultimately all that will remain of us, once we shed our body, is what we have done and thought. The same likewise applies, presumably, to the eventual disappearance and demise of all our culture's material artefacts. Here's Rilke again, in the seventh *Duino Elegy*:

Nowhere, my love, will world be but inside us.
Our life goes hand in hand with transformation.
Appearance dwindles more and more. Where once
a house stood solid, now each created form
spans across to all thought can
possibly create, integral to it
as though entirely of the mind.

In his poem 'An Arundel Tomb', Philip Larkin comes close to a similar perception. The stone figures of a couple lying hand-in-hand on a tomb containing their bones inspires him to suggest—though sceptic that he was, this statement is hedged round with the doubt and prevarication of a double 'almost'—that 'what will remain of us is love'.

'Humanity needs a knowledge', says Steiner, 'that does not relate to this earthly transience, but is connected instead with what passes beyond it'. If in the end our thoughts and actions—both loving and otherwise—are the only reality, this lends a profoundly moral dimension to our connection with the universe, and elsewhere in this volume Steiner focuses as always on human responsibility for what both the human being and the world will eventually become, which is far from a foregone conclusion. He wants to enlist our active participation in evolution, which is not something that merely unfolds physically beyond our reach. Even the way we think can change and affect it, the degree to which we can concentrate our thinking and picturing in meditation, infusing head thinking with warmth of heart. The earth will ultimately go under, but what we ourselves create remains, with all its future consequences. The brain, complex and vital though it is, is the corpse of the living human soul, says Steiner, while the latter evolves hand-in-hand with the world, learning very gradually to live in reality and free itself from the limits and confines of subjective apprehension. The 'workshop of the gods' was once upon our time in our head during sleep, but we have already freed ourselves to some degree from their work there and can now think for ourselves. Today they have set up shop instead in our metabolism and will impulses, of which we are usually so deeply unconscious whether awake or not. The form of awareness that can encompass and comprehend the will is one by no means easy to access, is removed—as much in this volume is removed—from easy, rational logic. But that makes it all the more essential for us to learn to work with the gods by trying to penetrate the darkness that can start to reveal its secrets by such efforts, and to approach a deeper, more intuitive understanding than we normally have of ourselves and the world with which we are evolving. Orpheus in Greek myth descended into an underworld into which Steiner also leads us. Rilke's last poem in his extraordinary sequence tells, firstly, of the pain of knowledge that Steiner likewise impresses on us in these pages, and of how, perhaps, to stand upright within it; then somehow, of a self-relinquishment that finds a truer unity with the world, the development of greater capacities that create paradoxical coherence in this deeper encounter:

> [. . .]
> In this unfathomed night, at crossroads when
> your senses strangely congregate, become the power
> that makes their meeting meaningful. And then
>
> when all earthly things forget your name
> whisper to the silent earth: I flow.
> Say to the flowing water: Here I am.

Matthew Barton, August 2016

Part One

LIFE OF THE HUMAN SOUL AND ITS RELATION TO WORLD EVOLUTION

LECTURE 1

29 APRIL 1922

THIS series of lectures was publicized under the title of 'Human Soul Life and its Relationship with World Evolution'. In our immediate experience of human soul life we do not directly summon this question of the human soul's relationship with the whole compass of world evolution. That is, it does not figure in us as a conscious question. But unconsciously the human soul does continually ask this precise question: How, as human being, do I relate or connect with the broad scope of world evolution in general? Basically, humanity's religious life has always arisen from this unconscious question in the depths of the human soul. You see, our more or less apparent religious connection with the eternal is in fact the expression of this unconscious question in the depths of the human psyche.

In our conscious awareness, soul experience involves, in a sense, feeling enclosed and shut off. Our feelings, experiences and memories arising inwardly in response to the outer world and its impressions are messages and recollections from that world in our feeling and sensibility, in our experience of its range of occurrences, our memories and so forth. When we look at our life of will and action, we can say that the impulses of our thinking, feeling and will spring from the deepest interiority of our being—from depths that are to begin with well beyond our conscious reach.

We regard our thinking capacity in relation to external sense perceptions, the thinking that lives also in memories, the will impulses that come to expression in outward actions as—all of it—something self-contained when we first consider our soul nature and try to practise what is ordinarily called 'self-reflection' or 'self-observation'. But deeper insight into our own being will immediately show us that this self-observation fails to satisfy our deepest soul needs, and that in our own profoundest depths we inevitably ask what in us is connected with an intrinsic and given foundation—something eternal perhaps—that underlies the transient phenomena that I perceive before me in nature and human life.

Initially we seek within our feelings, our sensibility, for the deepest roots of our own being. And from this quest arises the question, with either a more philosophical, or religious, or other nuance: 'What am I rooted in? This root that I feel within me, in what way is it embedded in something objective, something perhaps cosmic—in brief, in something outward that resembles my inner nature, in which my inner being is rooted in a fulfilling way?' Basically, our mood of soul in life depends on whether we are able to find some kind of answer to this question, which is of the utmost and inmost importance for the soul's life and destiny.

As you can see, this brief introduction shows there to be, in a sense, a contradictory element in human soul life. On the one hand we find a self-contained and enclosed quality in our thinking, feeling and will, but on the other hand this does not satisfy us since we also outwardly perceive how our bodily case or shell partakes of the destiny of other natural objects—arising, developing and decaying as they do. We discover that an outward mode of observation is completely inadequate for demonstrating any connection between our soul and the eternal, since this soul, as we initially perceive in outward ways, vanishes when life in the physical body ceases.

Our inmost need of soul initially contradicts, therefore, what the soul first discovers through ordinary, mundane forms of self-observation. But if we allow ourselves to dwell deeply and feelingly in this contradictoriness—which is connected with our destined inner experience of human nature *per se*—then we can look fully upon this surging, weaving life of soul and find that it bears two distinctive polarities within it: in one direction it develops thinking, and in the other, will. Between thinking and the will we find sensibility, feeling; and we become aware how the thoughts and pictures that we can say we draw from the outer world are accompanied by feelings and emotions, which give these thoughts and ideas the inner soul warmth that the soul needs. We become aware also, on the other hand, that the will impulses flowing from within us are connected for their part with a feeling and emotional quality, and that certain feelings and emotions cause us to form a resolve of will of some kind or other. Or that in other words we accompany with our feelings what arises from such resolves of will, so that we are either pleased and satisfied with what we will, or not. At one pole of soul life, therefore, we find thinking, and at the other, will life; and in the middle between these, connecting with both thought life and will life, we find our life of sensibility, feeling and emotion.

Turning our attention more towards thinking we will, if we are honest, have to admit that in ordinary experience our thinking is so fleeting in nature that initially it resembles what we experience outside us, all that our senses experience in the outer world. Certainly, soul life in a sense continues our sensory experiences, but endows them with a colouring, sometimes producing from within us memory pictures that have a quite different nuance and colour from the originating experience in the sense world outside us. Yet as long as we do not give ourselves up to fantasies and dreams but confront even imaginary things in a way that does not nurture illusions, we will find that all thought life is stimulated by our senses' outward receptivity. If we shut ourselves off to some degree from this outward sensitivity and, without falling asleep, dwell within our own life of thinking without activating the will, then all kinds of memories of external perceptions enter this thinking—transformed external perceptions. When in a sense we shut off all our senses and simply experience thinking within us, we gain a very clear experience of the pictorial character of what we encompass there. We feel that we have pictures of what these thoughts express. We even feel the fleeting quality of these thoughts: they surface in our awareness and depart from it again. It is not so easy to tell whether they are a reality or merely pictures. Or if we assume that they are based on a reality, we cannot at first grasp this reality because our thoughts present themselves as pictures. But this we know very clearly: when we live in thoughts we live in a world of pictures.

But what we experience in our world of will is radically different from this picture world—it is something that our ordinary awareness cannot penetrate. Ordinary consciousness forms a thought or an undefined, instinctive impulse: I want this or that, I wish to move my arm; and after a relatively short span of time the arm moves. The arm's movement is again apparent to us. We have two thoughts: that of raising our arm, and then that the arm has been raised. But we have no immediate idea of what has unfolded within us as will—it vanishes into the unconscious like states of sleep. As far as our will is concerned, we are asleep even when awake. Whereas ideas can exist in our ordinary awareness with bright clarity—bright and clear in our consciousness despite our lack of knowledge about how they relate to and are rooted in reality—the will lapses from our conscious awareness as it is enacted.

But in relation to this will we know something else instead. When the will becomes action, when therefore it is real will and not just wish, it expresses itself beyond all doubt in reality. First I have a thought or idea, and this is a picture: I will raise my arm. What then occurs is something ordinary consciousness cannot follow, and yet I do raise my arm. A real occurrence takes place in the outer world. What lives in the will becomes outward reality, in the same way that other natural processes are outward reality.

In my thoughts I have the character of image. Initially I do not know how the pictures elaborated as thought connect or relate to reality. But I am perfectly aware that my will is connected with reality. And yet I cannot grasp this will in bright clarity as I can with thoughts.

Between these two poles we have feeling, emotion, which colours idea and will. It partakes of the brightness, the luminous clarity of picturing on the one hand, and of the darkness, the unconsciousness of will impulses on the other. We see a rose and bring it to mind inwardly as image. Then we look away from the rose. The image remains as thought picture. As human beings we are not pervaded by absolute inner cold. We feel pleasure in the rose, delight in it. We feel inner satisfaction at the rose's existence. But at first we cannot say how this feeling of pleasure at the rose's existence arises. The way it emerges within us remains at first vague and indiscernible for ordinary awareness, but it connects with the bright, luminous clarity of thoughts. We can say that it tinges or colours our thoughts. When we have a clear picture of the rose, we also have a clear picture of what pleases us. The bright, luminous clarity of the picture of the rose within us is transferred to our feelings.

But when we have an impulse of will—we need only observe ourselves to discover this—it emerges from the depths of our being: I want or I will this or that. And how often we find ourselves instinctively driven towards something! Our thinking may often tell us that something really ought not to happen, and that what occurs displeases us. But when we contemplate our own life of soul, and enquire into our own feelings, we have to admit that the displeasing occurrence arose from a certain feeling, and was rooted in dark depths of the soul. We have to acknowledge that the origin of its quality and character remains hidden from us. This feeling quality plunges back into the same unconsciousness and darkness as the will. Our feeling therefore participates in very different ways in the bright clarity of thinking life on the one hand and the obscurity of will life on the other.

Thus our soul life appears threefold: as thinking and picturing, as feeling, and as will. But towards each of the two poles its inner nature is configured in an inwardly distinct and very different way.

Thinking points us intially towards the sensory world. It is true that we do not only admit simple sensory perceptions into our mind—such as red, blue, C sharp, C, G, warmth, cold, pleasant fragrances or unpleasant smells, sweet, sour and so forth. The ongoing flow of these sensory feelings can still be ascribed to the sense world itself. But what happens when we encounter more complex outer processes? Let us imagine for a moment standing in front of another human being: countless sense impressions are communicated to us from him. What we see in his face, and the rest of him, the things he utters, the way in which he moves—all the many simple sense impressions that reach us form themselves into a whole, into the way we then experience this other person. And so we can say that we experience the world through our sensory impressions and sensations.

Yet only sensations themselves are tied to us in a narrower sense: simple sensory impressions such as red, blue, C sharp, G, warm, cold and so forth stand closest to our soul life. More complex experiences—we could think of another person or also an entirely outward event—are also ultimately composed of sensory experience. We know that we are intimately connected with the red colour of the rose when it meets our gaze. But it is a more complex thing if, say, a mother gives her little boy a rose. This process detaches itself from us, we are not so intimately connected with it; and we only come closer to it when, perhaps through what we know of the Rose of Shiraz,[1] we recall something more complex that we have not actually seen, that we have only heard of by different means—in which sensory impressions no longer have a direct relationship with outer reality. We may have read the story, and then our sensory impressions were those of black letters, the forms of the letters on paper; or we heard someone recounting it, but such sense impressions point us to something that is very much detached from us. We can therefore distinguish between the direct, intimate connection that sense impressions have with our soul life and something at a further remove from us that is only mediated by sense impressions.

But something similar is also true of the other pole of human life. When I move an arm, the will is expressed and elaborated. Something occurs in my own organism. I am intimately connected with the expression of will that follows from my impulse of will. In fact, I am as intimately connected with it as I am with a sensation. But now consider this: if instead of just moving my arm I chop wood, then what happens through my will also detaches itself from me to become an outward occurrence. It is just as much the outcome of my will as the raising of my arm, but it detaches itself from me and is then outwardly present. Now consider how complex are the occurrences that can issue from such impulses of will! And if you examine these things more closely you will be able to compare what *enters* us on the one hand as intimate sense impressions that lead us to outer realities detached and separate from us, and what *emerges* from us as will impulses that detach themselves from a mere expression of the will in our own organism, becoming outward occurrences separate and distinct from us. Thus we stand in the world through the two poles of our human nature.

As we pursue these observations, we come to recognize the key difference for our soul life between what reaches us through the senses, what exists out there in the world, all that I perceive through sense impressions, and what emerges from me as will impulse and causes effects in the outer world, also existing there as reality. Both these are outward occurrences. I can for a moment think myself away from my sense perceptions and simply picture the outward occurrence existing separate from me. I can in turn think myself away from my will impulses and simply observe what occurred through me—these too are outward occurrences. I am related to the outer world in these two ways. But I am related there to outer processes that are separate and detached from me. In the outer world the one merges with the other.

Let's assume I'm chopping wood. First I see the wood in front of me. Or perhaps I see more than this—a complex outer occurrence. I see someone who carries the wood here to me, places it down for me to split. Now I am ready to chop the logs, to split them. My sense impressions guide me at every turn, with every blow of the axe. First I have the log, then I chop it, and now it has split into two. Without me it appeared like this [see drawing, top image]. It assumes this form [below] through my actions. My sensory impressions pass from one into the other so that outer events occurring through me, and not occurring through me, become an interwoven current.

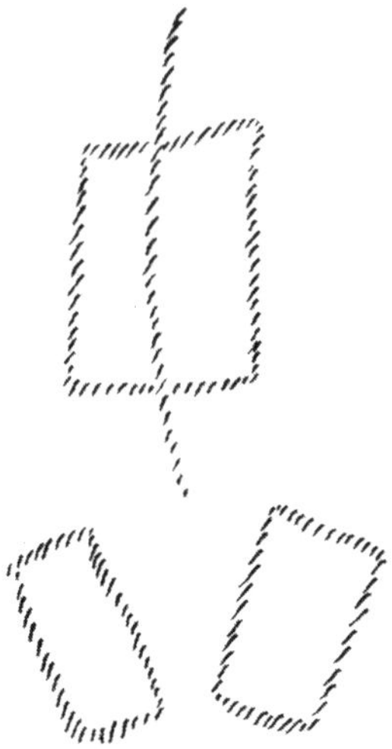

Try to feel how the enigma of soul life kindles from this simple question: how on the one hand I look upon the world as it already exists and on the other on what occurs through my actions. This characterizes the simplest outer fact of our soul's relationship to the surrounding world. Naturally this does not yet tell us very much, but at least we have brought the enigma, the problem to our awareness from a certain perspective.

But let us now do so from a different perspective. We have our senses, through which initially we learn about the outer world. We have our limbs, by means of which we enter into activity and movement. And basically everything we introduce into the outer world occurs through our will impulses, mediated by our limbs. On the one hand therefore we have our sense world, and on the other our limbs. And based on the whole set of circumstances we have described we can say that the nature of our limbs, the nature of our senses, are polar opposite. We can say that the outer world ceases in our senses before it becomes our inner world. And in our limbs an outer world begins which then detaches itself from us and streams on. This requires us to seek a relationship between our senses and limbs. You may perhaps be able to picture something very essential apparent in our human senses if you consider the eye, for it possibly conveys sensory nature most tangibly. The eye is a relatively autonomous organ, with its independent existence, sitting in its bony orbit. The life of nerves and blood in the eye goes inwards into our physical organism only as its backward continuation. There is a connection here with our whole organism, but apart from this the eye is relatively autonomous.

Here we see a whole series of physical processes in the eye, or at least processes that we can interpret physically. To speak symbolically, light approaches us, enters our eye and is there assimilated in a certain way. I do not wish to describe the physical and chemical processes that unfold there, for I wish to speak about soul life not about physiology. But I do want to draw your attention to how we initially have a kind of autonomous life in the eye.

We can in fact compare this kind of autonomous life with what happens in a purely physical model of the eye, an apparatus, a kind of camera obscura, into which light falls in a way similar to how it enters the eye. We can have certain processes that do not, however, live any longer in the eye, that do not, as they do in the eye, become sentient. But we can model and demonstrate certain occurrences through a physical apparatus. We can see from this that something resembling a physical process occurs in a relatively autonomous organism but does not come directly to consciousness. What comes to our awareness is the perceived outer object in whatever form and however illumined. What resembles a physical process unfolds unconsciously within us, unfolds as an autonomous process. This is only possible because of the relative autonomy of our organ of sight. This is less apparent in our other senses, and yet something similar is true of them all. But the eye, our sense of vision, is characteristic of this and enables us to grasp it.

We see how sensory perception is something relatively autonomous. Actually we can say that when we consider the processes at work in the eye itself [drawing, red] they are, right into the blood vessel and nerves, such a strong continuation, if you like, of what occurs in the outer world that we can model them physically in the way I have suggested.

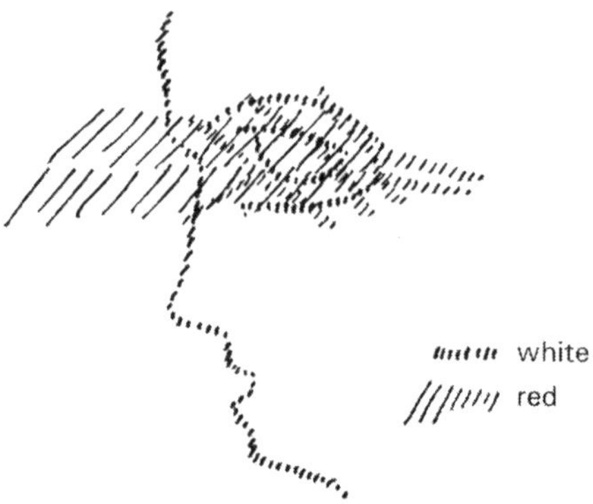

It is as if the outer world reached inward into the eye like an ocean inlet. What occurs outside us continues on, you can say, within us, inside our physical body. You see, that is one aspect of sensory perception—that the outer continues on into our interior; so that, in a way that we will discuss during this lecture series, our interior life, our inner activity, encompasses what is shaped inwards from without like an inlet.

But there is another side of sense life, which we can describe roughly as follows if we stay with the eye. I do not wish to speak of blind people now, but to consider the matter more from a general human perspective. We will then return to all these things from the intimate standpoint of anthroposophic spiritual science. Let us assume we were deprived of the world of vision. We can picture the lack we would have in our life of soul if we were deprived of what flows into us through the eyes. Let us just imagine what it is like if the soul within is dark because light cannot flow into us. As we know, darkness invokes fear in certain people, certain temperaments. People who go blind, or are born blind, do not consciously experience fear in consequence, but they do have an objective experience that resembles that of a person dwelling in the dark. The fact that states of fear are connected with an experience of darkness can teach us that our sensibility is connected with what enters us through our eyes. But we can also imagine that such feeling states also act upon our organic constitution.

A person condemned to a streak of melancholy by having to dwell in darkness, perhaps because of being deprived of eyesight, will transfer this melancholy to certain subtler structures in the eye. And we can easily imagine that we would not be as we are if we had not received into our organism what enters us through our inner experience of light and luminosity. This inner soul experience of brightness flows right through us. It continues within us, doing so to such an extent that we can picture how certain inner vascular processes in us, inner secretion processes or suchlike, occur differently because of the perception of light that permeates our organism, enlivening and refreshing it. Our perception of darkness likewise affects our inner secretions and circulation, though in a different way. Thus we can imagine, if we stay with a consideration of the eye, that besides enabling us to inwardly picture the processes and entities of the outer world we also owe to it a certain underlying inner state or condition—of our physical corporeality as well as our soul. In a sense we are what light makes of us.

But now let us turn away from the eye—which is a sense organ on the one hand, conveying to us pictures for our inner soul life, but at the same time also, through an experience of light and darkness, affects our inner state in all kinds of unconscious, instinctive processes, refreshing or dulling and dejecting us right into the physical. Let us turn away now from the effect of visual experience on our being, and consider our lungs instead.

The lungs are also connected, related to the outer world. They absorb oxygen from the external air and assimilate it. They sustain our life through respiration. Unless we are an Indian yogi we usually do not perceive the motions of our lungs and breathing. But we are affected by the lungs' action—by whether they absorb the external air in a healthy way or whether, for some pathological reason, they do not do so properly. How we breathe through our lungs makes us as we are. In ordinary awareness we do not perceive through our lungs, but by virtue of them we have something that affects the state and condition of our organism.

We can say of the eye—and of every outer sense—that it lives on the one hand in processes of sensory perception but on the other also in a subtler process, less accessible to our awareness. Through our experience of light or darkness, something also occurs in us that is less palpable and apparent, less defined than what happens through absorption of oxygen by the lungs. We know that we are what the lungs' assimilation of oxygen makes of us because it is a robust, strong, intensive and vital process. What the eye gives us, on the other hand, is a more intimate, more subtly vitalistic process alongside the actual process of seeing. And so we can say that an organ such as the lung shows us in an especially strong and palpable form something that is only quietly hinted at in the eye or another sense organ.

Now, though, you can read in my book *Knowledge of the Higher Worlds* and in Part 2 of *Occult Science* about exercises we can do to develop higher capacities of perception that otherwise slumber in us. We transform our whole inner being through such exercises. But what occurs through this transformation can, in our example, be characterized by saying that the lungs assume a quality that comes to resemble that of the eye. In higher vision, the vitalistic process initially recedes. We give ourselves up less to what the lungs make of us organically through respiration; instead we transform the lungs into a kind of sense organ—not the physical lungs as such but a subtler aspect, the lungs' etheric aspect. Without adding anything to it, we make the subtler quality of the lungs into something that resembles the eye. Nature has made our eye into an organ of vision, as well as the instigator of an inwardly formative process. The lungs, in our ordinary awareness, are first and foremost an organ that likewise forms us, but as we experience knowledge of the higher worlds we make them into an organ of vision too: we make their subtler, etheric part into a higher sense organ.

And if we experience this etheric nature in the lungs, only now becoming aware of it, we can describe them in just the same terms: we can say that the etheric lungs, the etheric body of the lungs, perceives and is thus a higher sense organ. And in bearing the physical lungs within it, it is also a vitalizing organ. You see, as we acquire knowledge of the higher worlds, the lungs change from being an ordinary, non-perceiving bodily organ—dedicated however to the body's growth and life—into a higher sense organ.

We can likewise make such observations of the heart, and of the other organs—kidneys, stomach and so forth. All the organs we bear within us can become sense organs through a certain process of higher development by virtue of their etheric, or the more spiritual quality of the astral, acquiring capacities of perception.

On the one hand we regard nature and our senses and say that the latter bear in them something that, naturally, conveys and mediates firstly sense perceptions and second our vitality. Then we look at our inner organs—lungs, heart and so forth—and find that these primarily sustain our vital functions. But by developing them through methods I have described in *Knowledge of the Higher Worlds* they become sense organs, organs of perception. And just as we perceive light and colour, that is, a certain portion of the external world, through the eyes, so we perceive a certain portion of the outer spiritual world through our etheric lungs, and a different part of it through our etheric heart. We can transform our whole organism into a sense organ.

You see, here you have in a sense encompassed a reality in the outer world that otherwise only penetrates to the surface of the senses and then becomes idea. This now approaches us more nearly, penetrates more deeply as external spiritual world. As we develop towards knowledge of the higher worlds, transforming our inner organs into organs of perception, we gradually become as transparent as the eye is. We see how the outer world permeates us.

But from this you can tell that if we stay with our ordinary consciousness we can only observe the external senses whose nature we have described. But can someone know everything about the world's cultures if he only knows three nations? No, for he has to be able to compare them. Just think how knowledge of the external senses is enriched if we can enquire into the nature of our inner organs when they too become sense organs.

This gives us a very particular and special kind of knowledge about the human being. We acquire knowledge of our underlying potential, and what can develop in us. But doesn't this point us towards something else? Doesn't it throw up a significant question? Oh indeed it does. If our lungs can become a sense organ through our own, self-instigated development, and if we can say that the lung is firstly a vital organ and then a sense organ, how does this relate to the eye or another sense? Today it is a sense organ but may it not once have been a mere vital organ at an earlier stage of evolution, and have developed, albeit not through the conscious process we undergo when we acquire higher knowledge? The eye may therefore have been an organ that served the organism in a way that resembles the lungs' life-sustaining action, without as yet being an organ of perception.

We can ask this at least to begin with. Since our vital organs bear within them the capacity to develop into senses, we can ask whether our senses may not have been elaborated through outward world evolution, and whether we might trace this evolution back to former times when the human being did not yet turn these senses outwards but when they were still internal organs, vital organs. In other words, compared to our modern external senses, we would have been blind and deaf, and our eyes—which would of course have possessed a different form—would have served a different function, as would our ears.

At the same time we see how acquiring knowledge of higher worlds adds something to an otherwise only outward knowledge of the human being.

Most of you have heard me talk from many diverse perspectives about the nature of the human being. These introductory words today have shown another, from which you can also see that the anthroposophic world-view can start from all kinds of perspectives. Only by compiling and summarizing the outcomes of all these different angles can we come to a comprehensive understanding of human nature.

People often imagine that anthroposophic research offers a straight path to a few definitions that are usually to be found in nonanthroposophic books about higher worlds. But that is not so. You see, what can be gained through just one perspective—which people often disparage, thinking only a single point of view is on offer—can be illumined from other angles, and then everything comes together into the whole, self-sustaining edifice of anthroposophy's truth.

Those who, in our materialistically oriented age, are used to basing their search for truth on particular precepts will say: 'Well, anthroposophy has no solid ground under it, whereas science is based on assured observations.' This is like saying the earth cannot possibly hover in space unsupported! Every planet must rest upon something if it is not to fall down. But this idea that everything must lie on a foundation only applies to earthly things, not to planetary bodies, and it would be foolish to apply what is true in earthly conditions to the different context of the planets in space. They sustain each other. And the same is true of anthroposophic truths: they lead us from the world in which we are accustomed to dwell into other worlds in which truths are mutually sustaining. It is vital to recognize here, however, that truths are self-sustaining.

These words today served as an introduction to the lectures I will give tomorrow and then next week about human soul life in relation to the evolution of the cosmos. I wanted to show, though, that what we can say about our soul nature with the aid of a supersensible method of enquiry takes its point of departure from what any reasonable, rational interpretation of ordinary consciousness can tell us.

This was therefore only a first step from an external mode of description towards describing how higher consciousness, as we can call it, observes the transition in the lung into a 'spiritual sense organ'—to use a somewhat paradoxical expression. On this path, over the next few days, we will continue to acquaint ourselves with the whole context of human soul life.

Lecture 2

30 APRIL 1922

YESTERDAY I spoke to you about the sense organs, and how we can regard them if, in addition to knowledge offered by ordinary awareness, we also include that of supersensible worlds. I said that the moment we raise ourselves to a spiritual vision of supersensible worlds then other organs—yesterday I spoke about the lungs—likewise become sense organs like our ordinary sense organs. This gave us a view of the organs in a process of change and development, of evolution. When we only consider the world in, let's say, mundane terms, we only ever obtain something that is fixed and static, its momentary state at present, and fail to discern what gave rise to this and what it will develop into.

We have to recognize the following. If, by simply raising ourselves into the world of Imagination, as I have called it in the book *Knowledge of the Higher Worlds,* we can discern the transition embodied in our lungs from a vital organ into a sense organ, we cannot continue to regard the lungs as we are used to doing in ordinary life. We have to say that our ordinary life shows us a momentarily fixed state. If we compare this current state of the lungs with that of our eyes, we can gain the view that what we find in our lungs is an earlier condition compared to that apparent in our eyes.

Yesterday I asked—and we can at least ask this—whether the eye was once a vital organ like the lung at an earlier point of world evolution. Let us stay with this, cautiously for now, as a hypothetical question. Let us say that it is at least a possible hypothesis that the lungs and the eyes relate to each other as, say, a young boy and an adult—that one is a younger, earlier form, the other an older form; and that therefore the eye might once have been a life organ at an earlier evolutionary period, and that the lung, a vital organ, could one day become a sense organ.

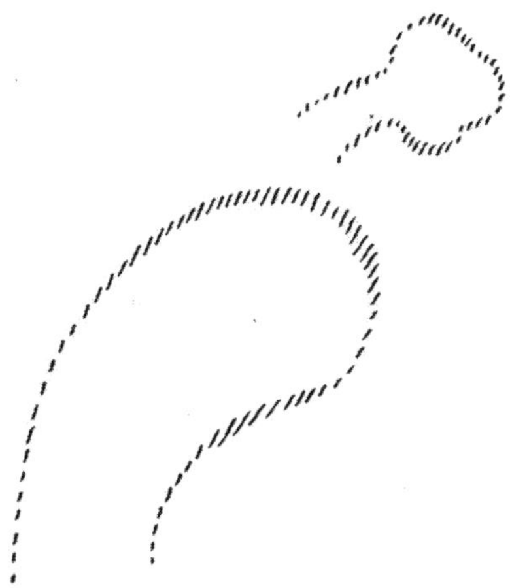

But the truth about this will only become apparent when we delve deeper into supersensible knowledge in this field. Today, therefore, let us consider the other pole, as we can call it, of human soul life, the will pole. Yesterday we described it in purely outward terms.

But now let us also consider the will pole by asking how it appears if we acquire imaginative perception. In doing so initially all our will organs grow pale: they pale before our spirit vision. The organs of our will are, firstly, our limbs; these limbs grow pale in our sight. And the characteristic thing then is that as we raise ourselves to imaginative perception and observe our external organism, we lose the limbs and the inner processes connected with them, the metabolism. We lose them in our perception. They are simply no longer present so strongly as they are for sensory perception. And if we compare all that we lose, in a sense, in this way, which withdraws from us in our higher perception, with what exists in the sense world, then we arrive at a very remarkable finding.

I'd like to represent this schematically.

Let us assume that here we have a person as we see him in the sense world {left drawing}. Now we start to observe him with imaginative perception. The limbs grow pale and fade away. But the whole skeletal system pales as well, and grows ever paler as imaginative perception increases.

Now imagine that I leave out here what grows pale in imaginative perception.

Increasingly I get the picture of the human corpse. But this means nothing other than that what remains of the human being after death, and what is then buried or cremated, ceases to be visible increasingly as one applies supersensible perception to the human being. Instead, something else becomes visible. Where the arms, the physical arms increasingly grow pale, all kinds of things become apparent instead. People who once drew on ancient, instinctive knowledge were far from wrong when they spoke of wings growing where we have our physical arms. Beings of spirit and of course the human being after death grow wings. But it is too crude to imagine this in terms of a symbol, a winged creature, a kind of better bird, rather than a living being of spirit. You see, if we pursue knowledge of the higher worlds further, rising as I have described from the knowledge of Imagination to that of Inspiration, we discover what this actually is, this fairly irregular form in the human being that could, crudely, be regarded as wings. It is far from easy to discover what this form one sees actually is. But if we study it further, gradually, through subtle observation we find out what it is, say, that appears in the place of right arm and hand, when I raise myself up from imaginative to inspired knowledge. Let me put this a little differently. To the horror of materialistically minded critics, the arms make a great many ghastly movements in eurythmy especially. People who don't understand eurythmy can't bear it. But if you observe the movements performed in eurythmy with Inspiration knowledge, you find that, rather than an isolated arm or hand, everything is present, all the separate movements are there. And because they all flow into each other, because there are so many of them, they appear as wings.

Now non-eurythmists also make a great many movements with their arms. All these movements, the forms of motion, the curves of movement, become visible [see drawing, orange].

Everything that is physical, the muscles, the flesh, the bones, cease to be visible, and instead their movements become visible. The same is true of the legs. But yesterday I said to you that we do not only move ourselves. To avoid ideas that relate to pointless activity I did not cite sport, but chopping wood. Here, when chopping wood, people continually perform movements, and all of these are present still when we rise from Imagination to Inspiration knowledge. But we do not only carry out actions through our body. We carry out the things we have thought, realizing them perhaps through others and so forth. All this starts to become apparent especially as we rise from Inspiration knowledge to Intuition knowledge. Briefly, in relation to the will pole all that we lay in the grave after death gradually becomes invisible while all that we have actually done begins to grow visible. And once we are dead, what remains of us chiefly is what we did. It is this that works on through life and has a further existence. What passes through death is like a birth of the will. And so you can see that we must choose another path if we wish to pass from the physical body to the soul in relation to our limb nature. Exactly the same is true of our metabolism.

Now I have in a certain respect considered the nature of our sensory system, as well as what can be called our will system, the nature of our actions. We can get a little further here now if we return to sensory nature, at one pole of human existence, drawing on developed Imagination and Inspiration to look back upon what becomes of a sense organ such as the eye once we live at a stage when, say, the lungs have become a sense organ too.

Once our lungs have likewise become a sense organ, perception of a quite different world begins for us—or rather for the higher human being who gradually detaches from the ordinary human being. Our ordinary nature is always present alongside this, checking what is happening—I have repeatedly explained this in public lectures too. But I'm speaking now of the person who is emerging, developing from the other. Now as soon as our lungs begin to become sense organ we also begin to perceive the world in terms of rhythm, experiencing it more musically. We experience everything I have described in *Theosophy*,[2] in my account firstly of the soul world and secondly of the spirit land. We begin to experience something other than our surroundings when the lungs become a sense organ. Yesterday I remarked that the lungs' etheric portion becomes sense organ. But what happens with actual, ordinary sense organs?

Of the limbs and metabolic organs we have to say that they fade from view. The sense organs do not fade like this, but reveal themselves to be as they are now. They reveal their spirituality. The sense organs become perceptible, become objects, but something like spirit beings. They are present—if I can put it like this—as something that henceforth peoples our spirit world. And in some respects we gain a strong sense, a feeling here, that these sense organs are enlarging themselves into the whole world, that a universe is being built up for us from our sense organs. This universe that is being built up for us now connects in our inner experience with something else. In our soul experience it connects with what we ordinarily think of as our memory pictures.

Here I need to point to an important experience which we have as we rise from Imagination to Inspiration. The sense organs become, in a way, autonomous entities, but at the same time they assume the contents of our memory. If we consider this, something of the nature of our soul life emerges very clearly before us.

Consider the human eye, which is initially an organ such as I described yesterday. Now, as we begin to develop imaginative knowledge, the eye itself does not disappear, but everything physical about it does. The eye becomes increasingly spiritual and we acquire a mighty content that is, if you like, expanded into the content of the whole world. But this in turn connects with the content of our memory [yellow], with the thoughts contained in our memory [drawing, p. 25].

By this means we gradually work our way through to a very specific insight. You see, modern psychology actually entertains a very trivial notion of our sense perceptions, in response to which, supposedly, we elaborate thoughts. And then these thoughts go—well, somewhere or other. Herbart,[3] particularly, was very enamoured of this idea that our thoughts disappear beneath some threshold, and that when we remember something again they simply amble up to appear in our minds again.

This kind of psychology always reminds me of a charming little children's game that I often experienced as an infant, in which a little mouse (the adult's hands) runs up the child's arm up to his head, accompanied by the words, 'The little mouse runs through his house, where will he rest? There is his nest!' In other words, an imaginary mouse takes refuge in a little nest which is located in the child's head somewhere. But our psychology has no greater insights, really. It sees thoughts as being stimulated by sense perceptions, which make their way into this little soul nest somewhere, this little box in the head, from where they re-emerge when they are recalled. This is a very banal idea, but one which modern psychology frequently resorts to. But only if we acquaint ourselves with the whole process through Imagination and Inspiration do we discover the truth of what happens. Then we will observe the following.

What knowledge acquired through Inspiration and Imagination perceives is not something it has caused. If you look at a piece of chalk, the eye has not made the chalk of course, for it is simply there. And likewise what is perceived through Imagination and Inspiration does actually exist. Thus as ordinary consciousness acts, this also exists as reality. All this does occur but can only be perceived through supersensible cognition, occurring in us in every waking moment. But the following shows us that as well as what we perceive in our ordinary awareness something else exists as well—that there is a parallel process at work which we only perceive when we develop higher awareness. Let's put it like this: in ordinary life everything we can perceive in our ordinary awareness is present, but as well as this there also exists everything we can only acquire through Imagination and Inspiration. In other words the latter is a process we are unfamiliar with in ordinary life. If we grow aware of it through higher cognition, it becomes apparent that the memory pictures we have in our ordinary consciousness are pictures whose reality only emerges in higher awareness. In other words, our memory pictures and thoughts do not amble back up into awareness having first descended and disappeared somewhere. When I form an idea in response to a sense perception, then withdraw from perceiving it, an idea now exists, and vanishes after a while. Since it is only a picture, an image, it has actually disappeared entirely. It has gone. But our senses do something else: they accomplish a process that we do not perceive; they vitalize the real process in us for our picturing capacity. When I have a sense perception, I first form the picture through it [red], but then a second process occurs [blue] through which something real is caused, not a mere picture. The picture vanishes and I no longer possess it. When I recall, remember, then just like the sense perception previously, this idea now works back up and I perceive the reality stimulated in me, of which I was unaware, when I first had the sense perception.

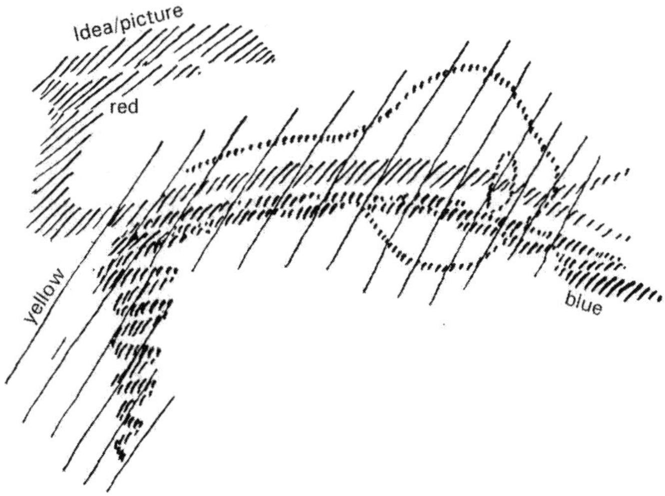

But this reality is soul nature itself. If you have a physical person before you, and you observe him now, and then again eight or ten years later, nothing physically remains of what he was ten years previously. You cut your nails, and scales fall from your skin—the physical body is continually being shed and vanishing into dust. And after a period of somewhere between seven and ten years, what is at present deepest within your interior has emerged on your external periphery and is shed as nails, scurf or scales from the skin. Rest assured that what today is somewhere within you will gradually migrate outwards and be discarded. This physical human body continually melts away. And what remains? The only thing that remains of the human being is the parallel process [drawing, blue]

that develops inwardly as the reality on which your picture or idea is founded.

After ten years you are nothing other than what you have absorbed and what has remained in your memory. You are woven from your memories; and of what was present in you ten years ago all that remains is what your memory wove from you. The physical has been shed, discarded, has melted away. If we take a rational view of what anyone can already be aware of by ordinary means, our ordinary healthy powers of reason can certainly gain the idea that things must be as I have now described them with the aid of Imagination and Inspiration.

If we now try from one angle—please note that we are now considering one pole, that of thought—to form a picture ourselves of the nature of human development in relation to the soul, we can only do so in this way [drawing]. First, when we are born, we have some kind of body [white]. This is filled by the processes that run parallel to sensory perception [yellow].

All this [white] is slowly discarded, shed. You eat, you assimilate all kinds of things through the air you inhale. This infuses your memory processes and keeps recreating your body. But the metabolic system that impregnates your soul is the aspect consigned to the earth after you die. Soul nature as such is woven from what the soul elaborates from processes that you initially feel only to be ideas, that you experience as ideas. So you can certainly say that you live in thoughts and continually create yourself through them. But what I perceive as thoughts in my ordinary awareness are only pictures of what I am doing, a kind of accompanying phenomenon.

Yes—but this gives rise to something extraordinarily important.

Basically, what occurs beyond the perceptions of my ordinary consciousness is far more important for human development. Consider the world. I take pleasure in what my eyes show me, what my ears let me hear. I experience all my sensory impressions. But while I am seeing, hearing and feeling, something slips into my interior that can later be drawn up again in memory; there slips into me everything that constitutes my soul. This is an ongoing activity: weaving, surging activity.

Someone who truly and seriously seeks to raise himself to spiritual insights can have a strong experience of what I am describing. When things are printed in black and white, people gladly store them away—they like to have this reassurance; people dislike uncertainty and so nowadays all knowledge tends to be written down in a way that can be easily pigeon-holed and stored for future reference. It is just anthroposophic lectures that people mostly find difficult to 'record' in this way. They are hard to pin down and therefore don't necessarily make for easy, comfortable reading.

But you see, this is a reflection of the actual experiences one has in relation to higher insights. A student who prepares for an exam today is very pleased if he succeeds in filling this organ of his with something. If he has crammed this stuff into him three or four weeks beforehand, and then arrives at his exam, he hopes to be able to pull out again everything he crammed in. This is not how things work with higher, supersensible knowledge. Someone who really acquires supersensible knowledge engages with living insights that do not behave as rigidly as the academic or scientific images of the world that, nowadays, people like to reassure themselves by writing down. I am putting things very radically because this points to a very important inner reality.

Let's assume that someone has acquired a fairly high level of supersensible knowledge. Now he possesses this. In processes I have frequently described he can draw upon it again at a later time, re-experiencing it, say, after three or four years. In the meantime, though, it has had a life of its own. As he again forms these insights inwardly, they enter his soul now in a way that is fraught with doubt.

One gradually learns to see that this is nothing unusual, that it is intrinsic to supersensible knowledge that, as it continues developing, as it grows old in a sense, it invokes doubt in us so that we have to recapture and regain its certainty by our efforts. In fact it is true of the highest knowledge that it can appear uncertain again the very next day unless we make efforts to reconquer, reacquire its insights. The kinds of knowledge that disappear, turn ghostly and then resurface again as they were are always of a lower kind. People look upon such knowledge and are pleased that they have gained higher insights that can be captured or fixed in black and white.[4] People like having a kind of blackboard inside them on which to record their insights. But this is not true of real higher perceptions, for these live, are alive. As one recreates them again, and this may be the very next day, one may suddenly be unsure about them after all, and has to recapture their certainty. This is a process one has to keep going through. In relation to these higher insights and perceptions we have to keep reminding ourselves that they are a picture of reality and not the reality itself. Very few of you will eat nothing on Sunday, 30 April because you ate perfectly well a week before and still have this in you. You won't refrain from eating because you are still being nourished by a meal you ate a week ago. Eating is a real occurrence and in this respect different from soul content of a physical kind, which remains in you and can be called forth again, in many respects unchanged or also altered. But this is not true of spiritual content, which not only fades and grows pale but is repeatedly fraught with doubt so that one needs to reacquire certainty about it. Yes, that is one phenomenon.

The nature of this phenomenon is really that when one has acquired supersensible insights about something or other the world seems to grow bright in consequence—as if one entered a brightly lit room, an illumined cosmic room. After a week or so certain residues of this remain within one from mastering these higher perceptions, working one's way through to them, so that they leave an impress, an effect, upon our physical nature. But intrinsically, out of their own very nature, they give rise in our experience to the sense of entering a dark room, and having to turn on the lights all over again. This image conveys something of the fate of supersensible perceptions in the human soul.

Someone who acquires supersensible knowledge simply cannot expect these insights to remain like remnant ghosts within him as is thought to be the case with instinctive, revenant-like clairvoyant ideas. These worlds one enters have to be continually conquered anew. But although reality will not allow itself to be stored away in our ordinary consciousness, the effect of it is preserved nevertheless. It is preserved in particular when someone who has supersensible perceptions has written them down or even—oh what a world!—finds them printed in a later edition of a book he wrote. Here he finds before him the external effect of what he once experienced.

I can call to mind associate professors who feel an inner, inward joy when they see before them this golden juice they have fabricated, when they can press one edition after another from this golden extract. This gives them pleasure. But the produce garnered from spiritual perception does not behave like this: it causes pain instead. You see, what is preserved, recast, decanted into the physical world, causes pain, hurts. That is the other aspect. Not only do we enter a dark room with our supersensible perceptions and must make light there again, but we also enter a room where arrows shoot at us from all sides, hurting and wounding us; and we have to armour ourselves against the residue, the embodied remains that we encounter there from supersensible worlds.

Here I am pointing you to a normal experience of soul life that we can have only by attaining higher perceptions. Ordinary experience is not such that we have a direct encounter with our soul nature, for we experience the soul mediated by the physical body, and it is adapted to this physical experience. But soul life as such is different; it is involved in continual development and change, in continual metamorphosis. Soul life escapes, evades us if we do not repeatedly live our way into these metamorphoses again; it is something we cannot endure because it is painful, because it dwells in the past. It hurts because it absorbs the past. When it is not immediate, present, it hurts; and one must arm oneself against this. But at the same time you will see that if we have had a real experience of higher knowledge, and have assimilated this, such knowledge is not so comfortable as what our students learn at university today. This hurts, at most, when they have forgotten it and do badly in their exams. And above all students do not find their knowledge painful but beneficial if they possess it. They are happy to do so. Their own insights will only cause them pain, if ever, later in life, when they see that there are better things than the knowledge they acquired, which has grown to be like fixed ideas.

If we live our way into the supersensible realm, knowledge comes alive. We learn to perceive how we must conquer and endure it. Through knowledge itself we learn joy, pleasure and pain, and thereby we come to know the reality of the soul. In ordinary everyday life the soul has succumbed so far to materiality that it appears in pale thoughts only, which we must first pour back into the warmth of feeling to rescue it from being pale, cold thought, which also causes no pain. This is composed only of pictures, which are not alive. But the supersensible knowledge that we acquire is alive, is living soul content.

And only this living content of soul can give us a real conception of what we are. You see, our memory pictures are a weak reflection of what we actually are. If we break inwards through this tapestry of memories, we reach what I have just described to you: a satisfying, delightful, light-filled experience of the world, as well as a painful experience of it, in which our soul partakes. Our soul is thus incorporated into a knowledge which itself contains soul life. The past pours itself into the pain. And what we feel to be joyful, delightful is what we come to see will pass through death with us—is the future.

Into physical knowledge a reflection of this must pour, but now a life-imbued reflection. History, and thus a retrospective view of humanity's evolution, as encapsulated in merely cold ideas about history, is simply picture, and only has meaning for as long as we carry it in our heads. Just as the ideas or pictures formed in response to sense impressions only have meaning while we carry them in our heads, and, rather than taking refuge in some little nestbox there, vanish when they are no longer present in our consciousness, so the intellectual ideas and concepts we form about history only have meaning for the head. As Goethe writes, 'What men call the spirit of the times is really only their own mind, in which the times they speak of are reflected.'[5]

We only become acquainted with the realities of history and evolution if we live our way into them through such living knowledge and perception: when we can experience the greatest degree of delight and sorrow in what unfolds in the world outside us; when, for example, we turn our eye of soul back to, say, the time of Ancient Persia, Ancient India or to Greek times; when we can gain a living sense of how differently the Greeks experienced their tragedies from how we experience dramatic works today. Goethe already made a primary distinction between Greek tragedy and modern drama,[6] saying that the latter is something much more dilute and pale. Greek tragedy was thought to have the power of affecting or changing world destiny. And so those who experienced it had a quite different sense of drama from a modern person who visits the theatre for amusement, and lets the events portrayed there flow over him like water off a duck's back. When a Greek attended a tragedy he felt shaken, deeply struck, and this worked right down into his physical corporeality. It was essential to him to feel his spine tingle in response to the events on stage. And in tragedy he found something like a remedy, for there lived in the Greeks the idea that life is imbued with sinfulness, guilt, and thus illness, and that public performances offered a remedy that repeatedly raised life again from this guilt and pathology into its truer, appropriate nature. Thus Greek tragedy was a medicine for the sickness that kept recurring in society, rather than a privileged and somewhat marginal place of amusement.

What is modern drama for people today? Well, modern plays may be a little more interesting than the latest hair fashion perhaps, but they amount to scarcely more than the art of the coiffeur: they speak mostly to the head. But Greek tragedy had much greater affinity with what a really knowledgeable physician does when he inwardly and dynamically infuses the sick organism with really effective, healing remedies and medicines. The Greek still appealed far more to the soul than do modern people. But when we consider history in this light, if we imagine ourselves into the inner state of an ancient Greek when he watched a Greek tragedy, then this gives us a view of history quite different from the usual, detached and non-participatory one.

If we study history in a real way, we convey our soul back into ancient times. In the modern world we suffer in a way you can experience if you leave here later without an umbrella and find it's raining. No great suffering, of course, but this modern suffering can easily give rise to something worse, so that you have to endure physical pains and discomfort. But we do not use any remedies to alleviate this suffering, whereas the Greeks did so. And if we really transport ourselves back to the era of ancient Greece, in anthroposophic terms we can say that we convey our soul there. We enter this era with our soul. To put it somewhat trivially, only in this way do we start to engage the soul instead of just suppressing it as you mostly do otherwise as a modern human being. You engage and encompass the soul, you learn to experience soul nature in your world-view.

This is what I wanted to describe to show how, if one seeks to reflect on soul nature, one must first draw it forth from its places of concealment; how one gets nowhere in this respect if we turn to mere images which we form of the world in our ordinary awareness, which psychologists then call 'inner content'. If you read a modern book on psychology, you will first find chapters on thinking as it figures in the ordinary mind, rather than how this thinking, picturing activity exists here below.

These books describe the thoughts and pictures extinguished at every moment [drawing, p. 25, red] and not what unfolds here below as parallel process. Briefly, if we consider the field of psychology today, it is roughly like a gathering of people, a conference where the most important people themselves are not present!

Let's imagine a conference of English people, who are very pleased to hear Lloyd George speaking.[7] But instead they fetch his portrait from the wall and put it on a chair, and thus he makes his 'contribution'. It would be the same with the French—they would have Clemenceau,[8] or the Germans their Bismarck.[9] Yes, these pictures are like thinking and picturing in relation to reality when described from the point of view of ordinary consciousness. They are merely pictures, and we need to get behind, beneath them to the underlying reality.

That is what I was trying to describe: the reality underlying these pictures. Soul nature is not present for us in our ordinary awareness but we must first draw it up from its hidden depths. That is the important thing. It is this we must keep in mind if we wish to speak of the human soul in its relationship to world evolution. If we properly consider the reality of soul nature we do gradually enter more deeply into the course of world evolution itself.

In these two first lectures I have been seeking to show you how esoteric knowledge and perception slowly encompasses and takes possession of soul nature. Having in this way created a healthy foundation for our reflections, we will, in as accessible form as possible, consider the connection between human soul life and world evolution in the next three lectures.

Lecture 3

5 May 1922

To pursue our reflections we will need to remind ourselves of a few things we are already familiar with in some respects, connected with observations made last week. Between birth and death our life can be subdivided into different states that we can consider from various angles. We have often spoken about the alternation between waking and sleeping and the intermediate state between them which is that of dreaming. These are the three conditions in which ordinary consciousness exists: waking, dreaming and sleeping. Yet these three conditions also figure as states elsewhere in the human organism. If we trace the contents, the experiences of our ordinary mind, we recognize the experience of thinking and picturing; and I have often said that we are only really awake, in fact, when and in so far as we are in this state of having thoughts. Anyone who observes himself with an open mind will be able to see that feeling is a far duller state of consciousness than thinking. Feelings surge through our soul, and we cannot relate them to anything in our outer surroundings or in our memory in as defined and precise a way as we can in thinking. We are aware, or can be, that during the moments of our waking life, these feelings come and go in a way that does really resemble the passage of dreams in the intermediate state between waking and sleeping. If you have a sense of how levels of awareness can be compared with each other, you will inevitably say that dreams are pictures; that feelings are somewhat like vague powers surging in us. In all other respects apart from the nature of their content, dreams come and go in us in the same way as feelings do. Dreams surface from a general, obscure and inchoate level of awareness, just as feelings emerge from, and sink down again into, a general inner condition in us.

The nature of the will is that what actually occurs in us when we have an impulse of will remains as hidden from us as anything we sleep through. The only clarity in will occurrences is the thought, the intention we have to act. And then again we see in our mind the movement we have carried out or whatever occurs outwardly through our will. But what happens in, say, an arm or a leg as we lift it, as we take a step, remains as unconscious for us as what occurs between falling asleep and waking up again. Even when we're awake, therefore, we also at the same time experience these three states of consciousness of waking, sleeping and dreaming.

But we only come to full insight into the human being if we make what I will call a rational appraisal of these given phenomena—of sleeping, waking and dreaming on the one hand, and will, feeling and thinking on the other.

If we compare the sleeping person with someone engaged in an act of will, we see that the sleeper does not have the content of awareness that otherwise ordinarily makes us human—the I experience. He has no sense of I. We usually characterize this by saying that between falling asleep and waking up again, the I is outside the physical person in bed.

And now let us consider the dreamer on the one hand and the feelings in us on the other. Ordinary self-reflection will easily show you that our dreams rise up before the soul as, in a sense, neutral pictures, and that these pictures that we dream as we fall asleep or wake up again hover not before—that wouldn't be accurate—but within the soul, weaving and floating there. What occurs here in the soul is different from what exists there when we are fully awake. When fully awake we know that the pictures we have can in a sense be held fast inwardly, that our human nature can encompass them—they do not float in such vague configurations as happens when we dream. We grasp hold of them with our human nature.

Let me draw on the board, schematically, what I have just described [drawing, left]. Here's a schematic representation of the human being [white] and now let us draw what we can picture as the schema for the weaving activity of dream [red], which approaches us roughly like this. The red shading I drew here is a tissue or weft that the soul experiences as continually escaping and then approaching again.

At the moment of awakening, we do not have such a weft in our soul experience but instead we now have something that we experience as within us. Let me now draw how things are in our waking state [drawing, right]. This weft or tissue that was outside us before is now within us: we encompass it in our body, and this makes it no longer a vague and fleeting apparition but something we inwardly master.

This relationship between what weaves and vanishes in dream and what lives within us as thought when we are fully awake and ourselves master the pictures and thoughts in our soul can become tangible to us—so that the soul really grasps this—as something that was outside us and has now entered us. In describing this we are actually characterizing nothing other than the entry into inner life of what first wove and faded in dream, as ordinarily apprehended, which we can call the astral body. Thus we can say that when we start to think on awakening, the astral body is within us, so we can think and picture, and know that we can control these thoughts. As long as they are dreams they hover and float outside us. Picture it like this: a kind of cloud in your proximity, interwoven with dreams. You suck this cloud in, as it were, and now you control it from within—it is no longer outside you, and therefore you are not dreaming any more. But just as you take hold of some object in your hands, you take hold of this dreaming with your inner nature. This means you have sucked in your astral body, and it is now within you.

But we have to ask more precisely what it is that we have within us. If we take a more careful look at what is there we may be able to find a clue by considering certain dreams that do not remain merely as pictures in us but start to become vague feelings. Some dreams are of course very unpleasant; they are simply a fabric of pictures. Some dreams are connected with states of fear and anxiety, and can cause you to wake up with a pounding heart. In these vague states of fear, and also often in vague states of joyfulness, though usually it is fear, you find the glimmering of something that develops further and is then present when we waken completely. What is glimmering through here, when a dream makes you feel fear?

Yes, the dream is interwoven with feeling. Fear is a feeling. The dream is still half outside us and therefore the feeling is vague and inchoate; and yet it does interweave with feeling, and enables the latter to manifest. But it interweaves with something else that lives in the soul in feeling. And only when your astral body has entered you fully do you have these clearer feelings determined in your physical organism, which can now pervade the astral body's thinking and picturing in you.

If you give proper attention to certain nightmares and fearful dreams, you can gain a tangible sense of what occurs as the astral body enters our physical body. What causes the fear or anxiety, and sometimes accompanies your dream, can always be discovered to be a disorder of some kind in your breathing.

From this it is apparent that the astral body enters and leaves us again through what lies in respiration. It really is not true to say that these things cannot be observed with an open mind. It is just that people do not engage in such self-observation. But there is something present in these phenomena which will help us to recognize that what weaves through our dreams and lives in the reality of the astral body enters our organism by engaging with the breathing process as we awaken.

This leads us to an extremely important reflection on human nature, one, though, which is rarely pursued. We usually regard the human being as nothing but an organism, a body consisting of solid constituents. But this just isn't true. The human organism is actually only ten per cent solid and otherwise is a fluid organism, a body of waters. We have to think of the structure of this organism as ten per cent solid [see drawing, white] but permeated by the watery or fluid element [blue]. And only then do we really properly conceive of the human organism—as a column of waters within corporeal solidity.

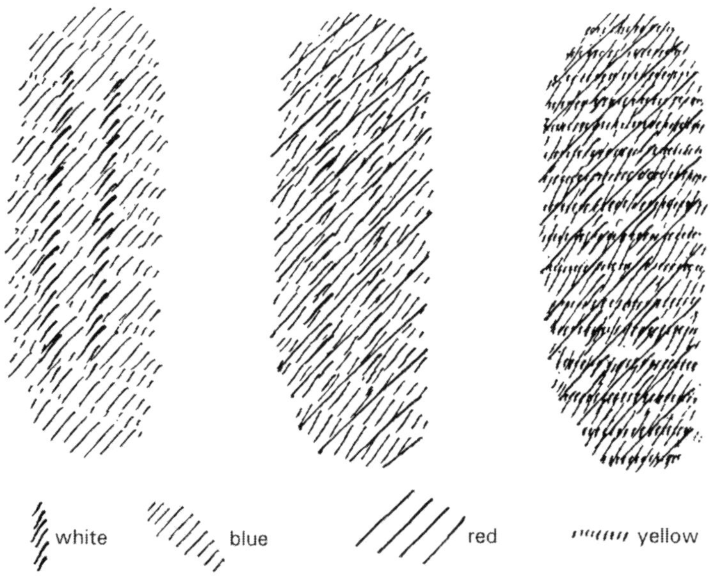

But this isn't yet sufficient. We must also picture the human organism as an airy or gaseous organism. Air is outside us and we breathe it in. And then a portion of air that was outside us is now within us; and then we breathe this out again. Let's draw this schematically [red]. It is precisely this air organism which the astral body takes hold of as we wake up. We breathe air in, and the air undergoes a further process: its effects pour through our whole organism. Oxygen absorbs carbon and is converted into carbon dioxide. This gaseous process continually occurs in us.

But when we wake up this gaseous process is pervaded by the astral body, by the same routes that air takes as it passes through the organism. The gaseous process is truly only that when we are asleep. When we are awake, the motions of this astral body swim in what lives in us as gaseous process. But now picture this: as the astral body enters into what I have drawn schematically here in red, and accomplishes its motions within the air organism's intrinsic flow, this occurs in what I have schematically drawn as blue, in the fluid organism. These air processes, which in waking life are really astral processes, keep pushing up against the fluid organism.

In the fluid organism, however, the human etheric body is at work day and night. And here you have at the same time a reciprocal action between the astral and etheric body, as well as the physical reflection of this: the air and fluid processes in us. You can therefore certainly picture these physical processes present in us, firstly, and unfolding between our breathing and the motions of fluid in us, all fluid processes at work in us; yet this is in turn only an image of what is happening reciprocally between astral and etheric body.

Now everything that constitutes our solid, fluid or gaseous organism is in turn permeated by heat or warmth [drawing p. 38, yellow]. The whole organism has its own warmth: warmth ether. We can say that the astral moves upon the waves of the air in us, and our actual I moves upon what plays through the organism as warmth.

Now you have the physical body as such: the fluid body that is also physical but distinguishes itself from the solid parts of the physical body (the fluid physical body that has an inward affinity with the etheric body); then the gaseous organism in us, which has an inner affinity with the astral body; and then warmth processes, which in other words embody the warmth ether in us, which has an inward affinity with our human I. In the physical realm, therefore, we find a picture of the whole human being everywhere. The solid parts are what exist for and by themselves, one can say. But the fluid in the organism cannot exist for itself. There is very little solid matter in our head, and what there is floats in the cerebrospinal fluid. If you study this fluid within the human head, you will find the etheric aspect of the head within it.

Now breathing occurs as follows: you breathe in, the breath pushes inwards and works on through the spinal fluid to the brain. In this impetus of motion, the astral, in our waking state, also moves at the same time up towards the etheric aspect of the head. On the one hand therefore we have an interplay of the movements of cerebrospinal fluid with those of breathing, and on the other an interplay between the etheric part of the head—the motions of the cerebrospinal fluid being only a reflection of this—and breathing processes, which are in turn only a reflection of the astral at work in us. And then we have a continual play of warmth conditions. And the motions of the blood mediate these warmth conditions. Upon this sway and surge of the sea of warmth in us, our I moves at the same time.

We need to picture this very vividly and comprehend it. Only the solid organism can be viewed on its own separately. The moment we approach the fluid organism, it no longer has any capacity at all simply to move like the motion of the sea's waves; the play of its motion, rather, is a reflection of what occurs in our etheric body. And in turn what occurs in the finer states of bodily respiration is a reflection of what occurs astrally in us. Now if we consider this, we must say the following: the cerebrospinal fluid has certain movements that reflect the etheric body. But we acquire this etheric body as we descend into the physical world from worlds of spirit. In worlds of spirit we do not yet have it. In encompassing our physical body we also possess our etheric body. We draw the ether from the cosmos towards us, as it were. And only once we have done this can we unite with the physical we are endowed with through genetic inheritance. Thus what lives inwardly in our ether body is something we already bring with us as we encompass and take hold of our physical body.

Let us now therefore picture the human embryo developing in the womb, and let us study the fluid part of this embryo. In ordinary physiology people do not do this, instead studying the embryo only in terms of its solid constituents, or at least what can be observed as solid. The fluid in the embryo is not studied at all. But, if it were, people would discover that the fluid, especially the cerebrospinal fluid, gives a reflection of what has descended into the physical body, slipped into it, and initially came to expression in the etheric body already, when this was drawn towards the physical.

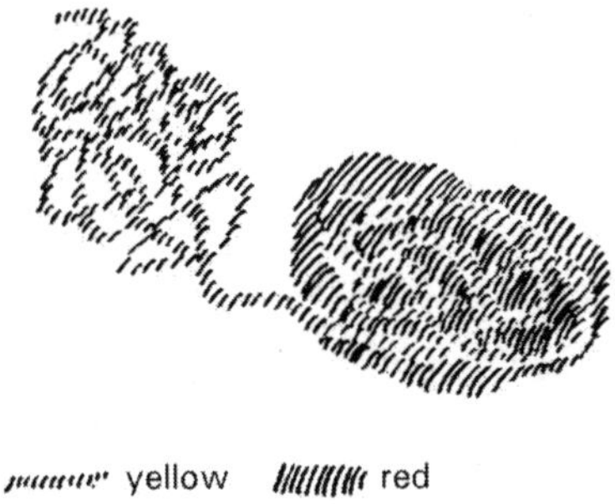

And so we can say this: here is the physical body [see drawing], the physical embryo develops—I'm not drawing anything solid here; this represents the fluid embryo [red]—with I and astral descending from the world of spirit. The ether that has already been drawn in [yellow] slips in here. By simply immersing ourselves in the physical body, what we bring in with us from without is absorbed in the fluid organism. If therefore you were to study the motions of the child's cerebrospinal fluid you would discover that this is really a photograph of what the person was before he united with his physical body. It is very important, you see, to be able to recognize that in the cerebrospinal fluid, or rather in its motions, we would find a photograph of what preceded conception.

Well, it is fairly easy to understand that the cerebrospinal fluid gives us a kind of photograph of what preceded conception. But now let us consider the breathing process. The process of breathing appears to us as a very physical process through the fact that our lungs show a certain kind of organization, that air is drawn into us, that the breathing process still continues under the influence of the outer world when we sleep, and thus when our eternal being is no longer in the least connected with our temporal one. Breathing functions just as well when we sleep as when we're awake. When we sleep, the wave of motion of the breathing process continues to pass through our organism; and when we are awake, this wave bears the astral body. This wave can sustain the astral, but also does not have to. In sleep it no longer does so.

What follows from this? Because the cerebrospinal fluid is enclosed within us, it can work on, can be a kind of perpetuation of what formerly existed. But this former element cannot in the same way be so inwardly perpetuated in our breathing. And therefore the following happens. If we study the human head and then the human chest organism, we find that inside the human head, in a sense let us say through the cerebrospinal fluid, and thus in the physical organism, we really do have a perpetuation of the pre-birth human spirit. This is not true of the breathing process. Here the physical process of respiration functions autonomously [see drawing, yellow] and the spiritual element is much less strongly tied up with the physical process [red]. We can put it like this. In the head the human spirit and soul is firmly bound up with the physical human being, so that they have become a unity. In the chest system, on the other

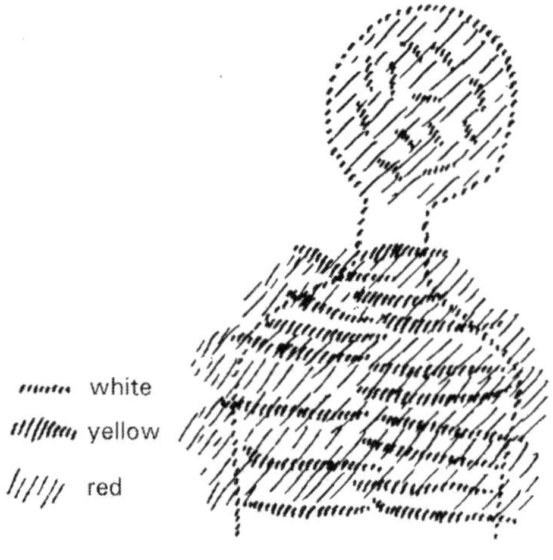

hand, this is not so, they are more separate. Here the physical organism exists more autonomously, and the soul and spirit likewise.

But now compare this with the dreaming state. As far as the whole human being is concerned, here again the I and the astral body are separate and outside us. But in our chest system they are always a little separate. The chest system, that is, our breathing and heart functions, our rhythmic system, is however an organism for feeling. And since the spirit and soul are not so closely bound up with the physical organism in the rhythmic system—do not inhere in it in the same way—feeling unfolds like dreaming. If we are trying to observe the whole human being, you see, we have to take account of these different kinds of interplay between the soul and the body.

A coarser view of human nature as it prevails in our materialistic age—and wherever you look in modern science you can find that the whole human organism is regarded as solid, with the soul somehow acting within it—will not enable people to understand how the soul faculties they experience, the pure inner experience, say, in an act of will, can manage to lift an arm or a leg. Compared to the soul quality experienced in an act of will, views of the human organism predominant in anatomy or physiology are as alien to the soul as a lump of wood. Physiological accounts of the human legs describe them more or less as two lumps of wood, two wooden legs. So how do they relate to the soul? Just as little as you could find a connection between two lumps of wood and soul nature, so you cannot find any affinity between physiological descriptions of the human legs and the human soul. But these human legs are permeated by fluidity; and here we arrive at something that enables us better to comprehend that spirit works into them. Yet this is still not easy.

Returning to the gaseous organism, to the airy element, we find ourselves in the physical realm in a materiality so fine that we can now more easily picture the soul inhabiting it. And this is even more true when we come to conditions of warmth in us! Just reflect on how closely we can relate these states of warmth in the physical organism with states of soul. If you have ever felt a terrible fear, you will know that you can break out in a sweat—and here you can see how the soul has an affinity with the states of warmth that arise in our physical organism. Briefly, if we grasp the whole human organism in terms of its solid constituents, its fluidity, gaseous aspect and warmth, we gradually come closer to the soul itself.

We can say that the I intervenes in the state of warmth, the astral body in the gaseous state, the etheric body in the fluid state, and only the solid constituents of the body remain untouched. These supersensible elements do not enter it. Now let us picture what exists in the human organism. Here we have the brain, but this is still fluid in nature. And now here are solid constituents within it—into which, as I said, the soul does not enter [see drawing, p. 42]. In reality these are salt deposits. The solid parts within us are in fact always salt-type deposits. Our bones consist only of such deposits. But inside our brain very fine, continually redissolving deposits occur. I would put it like this: there is always a tendency in our brain towards bone formation, towards the brain becoming entirely ossified; but since everything is in movement, this tendency is always dissolved again. In considering the brain we first have its state of warmth in which the air lives that is continually inhaled and exhaled but which plays up into the cerebrospinal fluid, and the astral body lives in this. We have the cerebrospinal fluid, in which the etheric body lives. And now we come to the solid parts into which the soul cannot enter. It cannot enter where we form salt deposits inside us. This ten per cent of our organism, this salt formation, means that we have in us something into which the soul cannot enter.

So there you stand, a human being, with your organism. Within it you have warmth, the gaseous element, the fluid element—and your soul can enter into all this. But you have something too into which your soul cannot enter. This is like having all kinds of objects here on which light shines and which reflect the light back. The light cannot penetrate the surface of a mirror and is reflected. The salt organism in you behaves in the same way—the soul cannot enter, and is repeatedly reflected back.

Yes, if you did not have this, initially you would have no awareness whatever, for the mind you have embodies the soul experiences

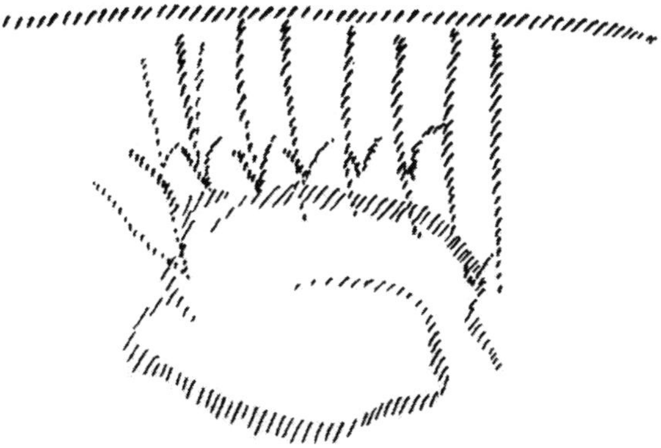

reflected back from your salt organism. You do not at first experience those soul experiences that enter your I, your gaseous organism, your fluid organism. It is only because soul life occurring in warmth, air and fluid is reflected back by the salt in the same way that light is by a mirror that you can experience soul nature. By this means you have an inner reflection that lives within as thoughts.

If a person deposits a lot of salt, therefore—but this salt arises everywhere in forms—then he receives a great many such thoughts and pictures; in other words he has a wealth of thoughts. If he deposits too little salt, his thoughts acquire very undefined contours, in the same way that a flawed mirror gives a poor reflection. We can put this differently too. If someone deposits a superfluity of salt, thoughts preponderate too strongly within him: these thoughts become very clearly defined but the person becomes pedantic. He believes, because his thoughts originate in so much solidity in him, that his thoughts embody something real. He becomes materialistic. If he deposits too little salt on the other hand, or let's say if he deposits too much salt in the rest of his organism and too little in his head, then his thoughts become poorly defined. He becomes a fantasist or possibly a mystic. The nature and quality of our soul life is, certainly, connected with material processes within us.

Sometimes, for instance, it is necessary to help someone too given to flights of fancy by giving him some kind of remedy that enables him either to deposit more salt or to better configure the deposited salt. By this means he can be freed from his fantasies. But the reverse is still more important. You see the curing, by physical means, of people's excessive fantasy or pedantry is not something we should take too far; and initially there is not much to be done in this way. But the reverse has great value. A keen observer of human nature, both physical and soul nature, will notice very accurately if someone has too many salt deposits in one or another direction, let us say in the head, or in the organs of the rhythmic system, or in the metabolic organs. He can detect this by remarking a change in the whole configuration of a person's thoughts, and the way in which his thoughts change can be very helpful for diagnosis. Most people, however, do not discern such subtle processes.

People very rarely notice, for instance, what it means if someone suddenly starts to misspeak a lot, to say the wrong words. If this is not usual for him, but he suddenly begins to misspeak, and this lasts a couple of days, we can see that he had a mild illness and this problem of self-expression is simply a symptom of it. Sometimes we can describe such occurrences very precisely.

Let us assume that, due to some passing condition, a person secretes too much stomach acid for a few days. What happens? The stomach acid of course begins to dissolve certain substances in the stomach, which should then pass on from the stomach. But now he does not have this further passage of substances in his organism, and he therefore loses the necessary sharpness of his inner, reflected images; now his thoughts become slack and he misspeaks. If you notice this happening, you can find a way of helping him to produce less stomach acid, and his thoughts will stop leaping all over the place and grow more regular again; then he will also stop misspeaking.

Or let us assume something causes too great an absorption of stomach acid—this might be due to abnormal spleen function. Thus the whole of him in a sense becomes stomach, and stomach acid is conducted everywhere in his organism. Such acid secretions are actually the cause of a great many illnesses. If the acid does not reach as far as the head, you can get very odd, prickling pains; but if it does, the head will grow dull. If you look at such a patient you can often see how he makes this whole assimilation of acidity into a form of greed—he becomes sour through and through. If this happens it will impair the friendly look in his eyes. You can observe his eyes in this acidic condition and, under certain circumstances, by giving him an acid that he does really process in the stomach, because it has no tendency to pass further into the organism, you can bring back a friendlier look into his outward countenance.

I say all this to show you that spiritual science, as intended here, does not attend to vague qualities of soul merely, but traces everywhere how the soul—which does really command the body, and is its architect and builder—works into corporeality.

We cannot comprehend how the soul lives in us if we regard the human organism as nothing but a solid entity, and fail to see how fluid, air and warmth in the organism approach the nature of soul life. The soul, you see, does not live in the solid constituents of the human organism. The soul enters this solid organism as little as light passes through a mirror. Instead it is reflected back, and in the same way soul is reflected back everywhere by the salt.

If this is our foot here, and here the bone, the idiosyncrasy of the soul is that it is repulsed by the bone [see drawing, red], that we bear our bones in us in a way that is devoid of soul. There is no soul within them, but instead it is reflected back into the organism.

Our skullbones are by no means badly arranged, for the soul, you see, radiates out in all directions to be reflected inwards again. We also inhabit our skullbones, but only as solid, physical human beings.

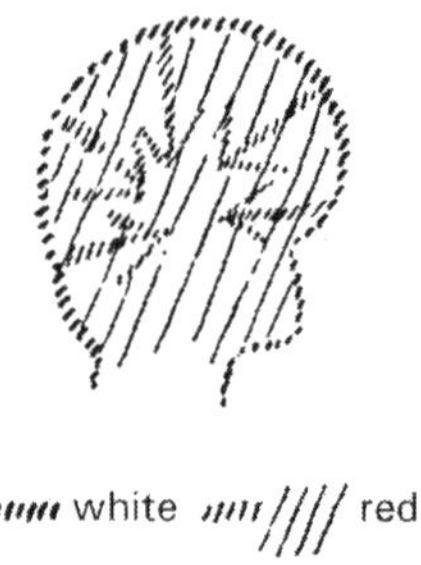

But our soul shines into us. And so really, if we properly depict our head, we must say that first of all the soul [red] spreads out within it. But this would leave us in a kind of dull, unconscious state. But where the skullbones are, the soul cannot enter, and is reflected back everywhere, into us [arrows]. And only when it is thus reflected do we possess it as soul nature or soul faculties. Within you, you really have your soul reflected back from all sides from the mirror of the skullbones. That's how it is.

Spiritual science does not discount material things but is actually what enables us to understand the material world properly. It shows how the soul governs matter. We don't understand a baker simply in terms of the movements he carries out but by virtue of the fact that these movements create buns and rolls. In the same way we do not understand the soul properly in abstractions, but we meet a picture in our organism of what the soul accomplishes. We must know how to regard this organism in the right way as a picture of the soul. If we do not have the will to engage with the human being, to study him fully in this way, also as we meet him in his physical appearance, and if instead we are content to see him only in physical terms, we cannot understand the soul either. You see, what is usually described as soul by those who do not wish to see the physical in spiritual terms has the same reality as if you were to place a tasty meal down here, and then a mirror here, and instead of eating the meal would try to eat its reflection. You won't get full like that. And likewise you won't grasp the soul without considering it as creatively active in all you do, rather than seeing it as image alone. In spiritual science we cannot despise or discount matter, but have to comprehend the material world spiritually, and then it becomes pervaded by spirit. Otherwise we live in abstractions, in intellectualism, which lead us away and not towards true knowledge.

Lecture 4

6 May 1922

YESTERDAY I was keen to show that the human soul is an active entity, and how, as such, it creatively, actively penetrates the human organism. Whenever we reflect upon the human soul we must also be clear that we gain sight of the soul whenever we grasp the outward appearance of the human organism in its totality as an expression and also—in so far as this organism is a mobile organism and undergoes inner changes—as a creation of the human soul. But this is only one aspect of soul life, and today we will begin to look at the other.

Firstly, recalling what I elaborated already in the first sessions of this cycle, let us consider our relationship with our surroundings. You will have to acknowledge that our soul is separate from the creatures, beings and objects we contemplate around us. We cannot say that we are inside the chair we're sitting on or inside the table standing before us. We regard the external aspect of these things. But at the same time that our soul life stands outside these outer objects, so likewise it is outside a part of our own organism.

To understand this you need only think very clearly and carefully for a moment about what we have often discussed in relation to will impulses. As I said, we first have the thought or picture of intending to raise an arm. Then after this thought has in some way vanished, our organism manifests the phenomenon of the raised arm. But what occurs in the organism following the presence of the thought picture—I can't even say after the thought has taken effect, since this effect is no longer within our ordinary awareness—up to the moment when we can see that the arm has been raised is initially outside the human soul, in fact is as much outside it as the table or chair. I do not enter into the table, nor into what happens when an act of will occurs.

But as soon as supersensible knowledge dawns in us, we can discover what is actually happening here. In our ordinary awareness we perceive the external aspect of things with our senses, the colours, tones, temperatures and so on; and they work on in the thoughts and pictures we form of these things. This is what happens when we look outwards.

When we look inwards, we first become aware that we have retained ideas about things we have observed, thoughts and pictures that surface again—or at least this is how it seems. We have seen that this is not how it is, but we can describe it like this for our ordinary awareness. These ideas are imbued with feelings that rise up out of our being in a dreamlike way. In other words, here too we glimpse a world when we gaze inwards, a world that comes to meet us from within in the same way that colours, tones come towards us from the outer world. Here likewise we stand before something outside us, in the same way that we stand outside outward things that approach us.

But when we rise to higher knowledge these experiences change, both the outer and the inner one. When we raise ourselves to higher knowledge in the way I have often described in lectures and in the book *Knowledge of the Higher Worlds*, we first come to Imagination and then Inspiration knowledge. You are probably familiar with all this. Now when we first rise to imaginative perception, and then inspired perception dawns, what we can regard as 'standing outside things' changes both in relation to the outer world and to inner phenomena.

As regards the outer world, imaginative perception first leads us to pictures. If we handle these pictures in the right way, they become pictures of the spiritual world surrounding us. Then inspired perception must take hold. Through Inspiration we acquire knowledge of outer spiritual reality that surrounds us in the same way that colours, tones, temperatures and so on surround us in the outer world of the senses. In meeting this whole world, which is now an outer spiritual environment, we must always remember that this is something other than ourselves. We arrive at the point of discerning elemental beings, the beings of the higher hierarchies in these spiritual surroundings; and they are different from us, other than we are. While we increasingly learn to see ourselves as spiritual beings, we also learn to distinguish ourselves from all the beings that are different from us.

But as we practise exercises that on the one hand lead us to perceive the spiritual environment outside us, we also make inner progress, make inner advances. And the inner discovery we first make is that we learn, in a sense, to regard our head with its knowledge as of very little soul worth. Of ever greater value, by contrast, appears the kind of knowledge that is concentrated more in the heart—though this is less the physical heart itself than the etheric and astral heart. We now become strongly aware of the etheric and astral heart, and here, very significantly, something, gives rise to bright, luminous knowledge.

,,,,,,,, white ////// red

I can sketch what a person can perceive here in roughly the following way [see drawing]. Let us assume that this is the human heart [red] and above this everything we value so highly in terms of our perception of thought life on the physical plane [white]. A person also feels this in the head, this weaving thought. Before we rise to higher knowledge, and when we attend to our whole nature, we feel these thoughts to be, let us say, an extremely refined part of our being. These thoughts are not greatly concerned with our own personal concerns. If you take the thought of a triangle, you can entertain it without this Lord Thought being all too concerned with whether I have a headache or stomach ache. Thought is really largely indifferent to my personal mood at the time. Likewise, whether I am sad, happy, in pain or feeling well, the thought of the triangle can hold sway in my head consciousness with a certain refined nonchalance, and pays little heed to my subjective condition. This is why people mostly concerned only with their subjective feelings usually fall asleep immediately if one speaks of thoughts bearing no relation to their subjective experience.

Well yes, in a sense this world so blithely unconcerned with our subjective condition is elegant and refined. But if we mix our subjectivity into this world, feeling ourselves close to our own nature and being, then this feeling does pass through the heart; you can say that it shines from the head down into the rest of us, then rises up again from below [arrows]. But what rises from below?

All our feelings, instincts, drives, passions. Everything of this kind rises up and rages, one might say [red arrows]. This surges up. Here we have something in us that is fully subjective; yet all that surges upwards of this kind contains the organism's whole simmering and seething. What has simmered in the intestines and stomach, and anywhere else in us, rages up with these drives and instincts, rises to meet us. And so we can say that a refined, elegant world exists up above; this is very genteel but it does not become soul nature in us at all since it is blithely unconcerned with subjectivity. Ultimately is does not matter who conceives the thought of a triangle or a lion, whether it's Mr Smith or Mr Jones. Thoughts are unconcerned with subjectivity. Soul quality only arises when something flows forth from within us that permeates these thoughts with a feeling or instinctual quality. If Smith is a hero, for example, and has the thought of a lion, then feelings pulse up in him from below of a kind that banishes his fear of the lion. If Jones is a coward who runs a mile if he even thinks of a lion, then that is the subjective element. But the thought of the lion itself is universal, and as such has no soul element but is only spiritual. By virtue of the instincts that rise up from within to meet us, the thought becomes imbued with soul quality. And this also makes the thought of the lion soulful, whether it inveigles Smith into thinking of the weapon with which he will attack the lion or defend himself, or whether it makes Jones think of the best way to escape as fast as possible. In ordinary life, this is what endows things with soul quality. And we can say, in a sense, that the soul always shines into the spirit.

Yes, but when you rise to Imagination and from there to Inspiration, things become different. Then you will find you have great difficulty initially in holding back drives and instincts and preventing them from coming to expression; they will surface in you in a much clearer, because now unadorned, fashion. They should not come to expression, they must be pushed back. But something else also surfaces. These thoughts stimulated by the outer world, which have settled in your head in such a genteel manner, come to meet you now through the heart, which in a certain way becomes a wonderful sense organ. The heart expands to be as large as the whole blood system, becoming a great, etheric sense organ. Instead of what lives in instincts and drives, a sum of thoughts [white arrows] now rise up to meet the thoughts above. But these thoughts are mighty pictures, and do not in the least express any more what otherwise rises from our organism. Instead they express what we were before birth.

We learn to know ourselves, to perceive ourselves, in the world of spirit before we were born here on earth, or before we are conceived. This comes towards us. Instead of drives and instincts, something else comes towards us when we develop imaginative and inspired knowledge: we are transported into our existence in the world of spirit before we descended to physical incarnation. And in learning to perceive ourselves in this existence we grow familiar at the same time with something that is different, to the eye of imaginative and inspired perception, from the outer world that ordinarily surrounds us. We encounter elemental beings, angels, archangels and so forth. Wisdom teaches us to know ourselves in our expanded being above and beyond earthly existence.

But this gives us very important insight into soul experience. We gradually see that this soul experience has entirely poured itself out in our head; it entirely inhabits the head and has formed the head as its reflection [see drawing, blue]. This now offers itself to the outer world so that these pictures we receive and retain in memory can paint themselves there. But here below this life exists without—as I suggested yesterday—uniting so strongly with the physical; here it is more detached. And so, when the heart becomes the eye for this downward gaze, we can gaze down into ourselves to this aspect, into the flaring, bubbling, burning emotions, desires, passions and drives

on the one hand, and on the other, though, to what does not want to unite with it, and is our eternal being living alongside it.

And now we can see that for our head the soul element is buried in it, rests in it. The head is really only an organ of reflection for our physical surroundings. We grasp only the outer world there. We grasp ourselves when we look deeper into ourselves through the heart. Ordinary life, though, only throws up waves of emotions. But if we learn to perceive more here through higher knowledge, we find our eternal being opening up. And now the soul learns to be united with the spirit that we ourselves are. What we glimpse through our heart as it becomes a sense organ is we ourselves, our own intrinsic being. The external world we observe as spiritual environment is not us. What we glimpse within through our heart, which becomes sense organ, is our own being. The path that otherwise leads us only into soul nature, its outer aspect of drives and desires, this same path leads us into the eternal soul that indwells us and is permeated by spirit, and is just as spiritual as our spiritual environment. So now we enter the realm where the soul is one with the spirit.

However much you look back at your brain, it remains physical; there you yourself are physical. But the brain is also the chief domain of modern, materialistic psychologists. When you say you are studying the psyche in fact you are only considering the brain. And you can do so because the brain is an expression of the soul: the soul is buried in it. This soul corpse is the domain of modern psychology. But intrinsically the soul as such, united with the spirit, lies below the heart; and here it is not intimately bound up with drives, desires and so on, but only outwardly related to them.

But now we can make another discovery. Let's take any sense, say the eye, vision. Firstly you look around you physically. Let's overlook the fact that we are usually in artificial light. We could easily demonstrate that this too has something to do with sunlight, albeit at one remove, but that does not concern us for now. Let us merely picture a beautiful morning in the country, outside in the sunshine instead of under this dreadful electric light. Let's imagine it—occasionally it happens! We see the sun everywhere, since the sun is not just a disc or sphere but radiates, and when its rays fall on a flower they are reflected towards us. It is the sun that penetrates our eyes, and enables us to perceive the flower, and form a picture, an idea of the flower. Everywhere, on every object, it is the sun that enables us to do so. But that is easy for everyone to understand—that we see the illumined objects around us by virtue of the sun, which, via our head, conveys to us all that we know in outward, physical terms about these objects. But what the eye perceives is not only the sun. There is a deeper truth to the lines in *Faust* about 'The sun in ancient guise competing with brother spheres in rival song . . .'[10] Such universal harmony does exist, and the aspect of this universal harmony manifesting in our atmosphere is also a sun reflection, so that in a sense all musical resonance also reaches us circuitously from solar nature. Everything we perceive in the outer physical world originates with solar powers: warmth, tone, everything reaches us from the sun, though not so directly as light.

And now I must tell you something that will naturally seem surprising at first sight, and initially incomprehensible. But we can gain understanding of it if we study things in the way we are used to doing in anthroposophy. We are actually within sun nature in what we see outwardly due to the presence of the sun, and through our sensory connection with what the sun enables us to see in the outer world. We inhabit the outward, physical and etheric sun nature.

If we now attain imaginative perception, and inspired perception—if I may put it like this, but we have to understand this only in the sense I just described—and if we now penetrate further into our own being and nature through our heart, this sun nature becomes something different. At a certain point where Inspiration arises, when we live actively with inspired knowledge in a real world of pictures, we acquire a sense that we have suddenly been poured into the sun itself, as if through an inner, soul-spiritual impetus.

This is an experience whose importance you should again dwell upon. The sun shines down upon us on earth. We human beings perceive what is around us as reflected rays of sunlight, sun nature. But the moment we gain knowledge through Inspiration, when the heart becomes an organ of sense perception for ourselves, as I described, we suddenly feel ourselves to be within the sun. We no longer feel as if we are looking up and seeing the sun move across the heavens—I'm speaking of its apparent movement—but, when the heart becomes a sense organ, we feel our heart to be within the sun and travelling within it. For our experience, simultaneously, the heart becomes transported into the sun, and the sun becomes the eye with which we now view what begins to surround us. The sun becomes our eye, our ear also, and organ of temperature too. We no longer have the sense that we are outside solar nature but that we have moved suddenly into it and now stand within the light. Otherwise we are always outside the light. Now, having plunged with our own being into our heart, we have a sense of standing within the light, of our own being as light. With our organs of light, which we now have in the surging, weaving light, we touch beings of spirit. With our soul we now have an affinity with a world that is not outside the sun but within it, and I will say expressly that we become linear; we feel ourselves as if on the path of the sun, on the sun's path with a linear quality. And if higher knowledge now advances just a little further, we not only feel ourselves to be inside the sun but in a sense beyond it [see drawing]. Formerly we were a little human being here below and looked up to the sun. Now we have entered the sun, feel our soul being to be within the sun, and the world that before was around us [green] is now inside us.

But only when we have achieved this do we begin to understand that when we sleep in ordinary earthly life our soul goes out there. We come to the place where our nature becomes such that we really only perceive through the sun. Now with our soul we go out into the world that can only become clear to us through the sun's reflection; and this is why we perceive nothing there. We would need to be transported beyond the realm of the sun sphere. But this only occurs through Inspiration, later through Intuition. Here we first perceive something because, as earthly human being, when we depart from our physical body and our etheric body, in a sense we squeeze ourselves through all earthly objects. From falling asleep to waking up,

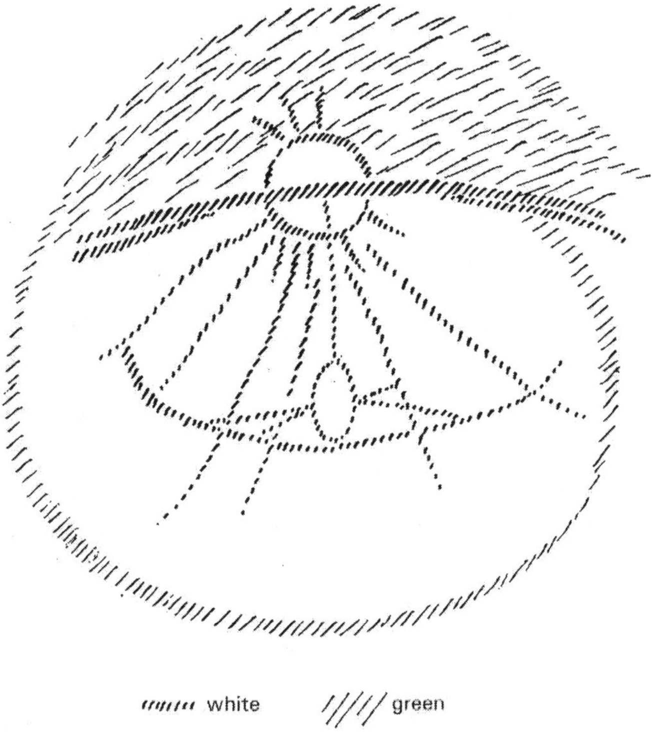

we squeeze ourselves through all possible earthly objects, and here there is little of ourselves to be perceived initially. We perceive other beings, but only when we have oriented ourselves accordingly. We can only begin to perceive ourselves when, through esoteric schooling, we emerge in the realm in which we were between death and rebirth.

What actually separates us from this realm in which we live between death and a new birth? Well, we cannot say that it is anything other than the sun. We are born into the physical world as human beings. Before conception, before we descended, we have nothing to do with the outer, physical sun, but only with the spirit underlying it. Now we descend into the physical world and the sun shines everywhere upon it. We absorb into our thoughts and ideas what the sun makes physically visible to us. This physical sun prevents us from seeing the spirit. And when, after falling asleep, we are outside amongst all objects that the sun otherwise makes visible to us, we are too weak—because we become so accustomed to earthly life with our physical body—to look out beyond the sun realm. And in the sun realm itself we can discern nothing for then we would have to see the other beings that surround us—whether elemental spirits or spirits of the higher hierarchies.

This can also be seen in terms, firstly, of a potential capacity to perceive the soul through higher perception than that of ordinary consciousness and, secondly, of the inner affinity of this soul with what exists as the world. The soul is connected with the whole of cosmic evolution; and when we are in our body it is the sun that renders everything outward visible to us, also renders things audible and so forth, but at the same time prevents us from looking out into the world of spirit. When we rise to the world of spirit, we arrive on the other side of the sun. Here, we are on this side of sun being; and when we advance towards the world of spirit we come to the other side. And in the transition from one side of sun life to the other, we become aware, as I have just described, of feeling ourselves in the sun, with the sun, passing with it upon its paths through the cosmos and so forth. We cannot become properly acquainted with our soul at all unless we consider it in intimate connection with the whole of world evolution, with the whole cosmos.

It is our physical body oriented to outward sun nature that isolates us, if you like, at a particular location of the earth and prevents us from uniting our soul with the universe. Our organism is what isolates us. The human being really lives in solar nature. And as you know, moon nature is mingled with it, if we consider purely outward realities: the sun shines upon the moon. In bright, moonlit nights, the moon reflects sunlight. We have sunlight from the moon. That is, we have a kind of shading or we could say 'less brightening' of the world in everything which now enters the world under the influence of moon nature.

Now, not only does the silvery moonlight enter the world, reflecting on objects in a mistier, dimmer way compared to their sharp, defined outlines in sunlight in the daytime. Not only does this reflection of sunlight come towards us from objects, but moon nature also lives in the earth by virtue of plants' and creatures' capacity for reproduction on earth. Moon nature lives in everything that can reproduce, and is therefore connected with powers of heredity.

If we were only subject to the influence of sun nature, we could still be human beings on earth, but we would be unable to bring forth another human being, to reproduce. If only sunlight existed the earth would, we can say, embody a permanent condition—no creature would die and none would emerge. There would be no heredity or reproduction. So we can say that sun nature on earth is the primal physical potency. It impels our soul towards the human head aspect, and there makes everything into picture. We only become real in ordinary soul life through our drives, our emotions, and in higher soul life when we gaze through the heart to see spirit, but also when we reach a realm beyond the sun. Thus sun nature is the primal potency in the sense world, we can say. But moon nature is mingled with sun nature in world evolution so that the latter does not hold sole sway, so that this sun nature does not engender a permanent condition, so that all plants do not live for ever but die and bring forth new ones; and all animals, and human beings likewise reproduce and die. Thus moon nature is also integrated into humankind.

Moon nature is always at work when a new human being enters the world. Here sun nature does not, in a sense, only reach the surface but penetrates into the interior of a person and shuts him off from a certain sphere. This is one aspect we need to remember. There is the mighty sun power, as we can call it, and cast out from this a certain portion of our outward world evolution, into which moon nature enters.

If I draw this human condition schematically [drawing, p. 62], we must say that moon nature would integrate itself into the human schema [orange] like this. Here, in so far as this sun nature participates in it, it is cast out and moon nature holds sway. So you see, something is taken from the primal powers of sun nature in the outer physical world. And so what occurs as moon nature here cannot

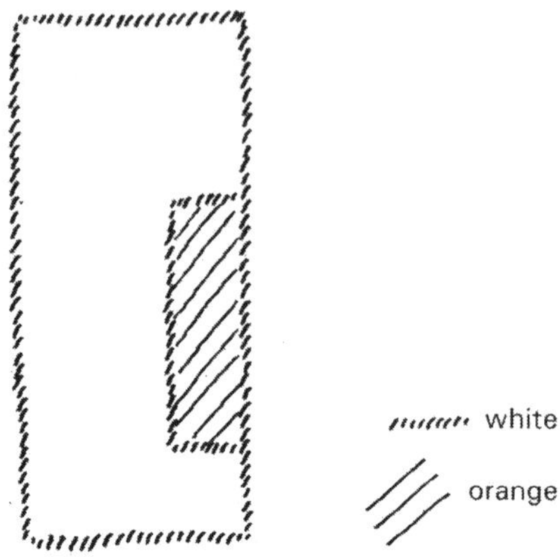

occur outwardly in the world in reproduction—or only partially in the lowest creatures, when eggs are laid and the sun hatches them. Specifically where moon nature grows very strong, it withdraws from the external world.

But there is a counterpole to this. What is withdrawn from the sun on the one hand, enabling earthly reproduction and heredity to occur through moon nature, is in turn given back. And this giving back means that the sun is not merely the physical entity that external science describes, but it has a spiritual nature, a kind of higher sun that belongs to it {drawing p. 63, orange}. This higher sun also belongs to the sun, but it acts upon human beings like the moon does, the latter being a kind of lower sun. And in our era people know nothing sensible about the way in which the moon is integrated into earth's evolution; and they know still less about this higher sun, and that just as the moon exerts a mighty influence on our physical nature so this higher sun very greatly affects the human soul.

In olden times people knew this through their instinctive powers of clairvoyance. When they sought to speak of this in regard to especially spiritually gifted human beings (people truly gifted for spiritual realities) they said that the higher sun was acting upon them, and that, briefly, they were not merely as they were through sun and moon but, by virtue of the higher sun, they were more than

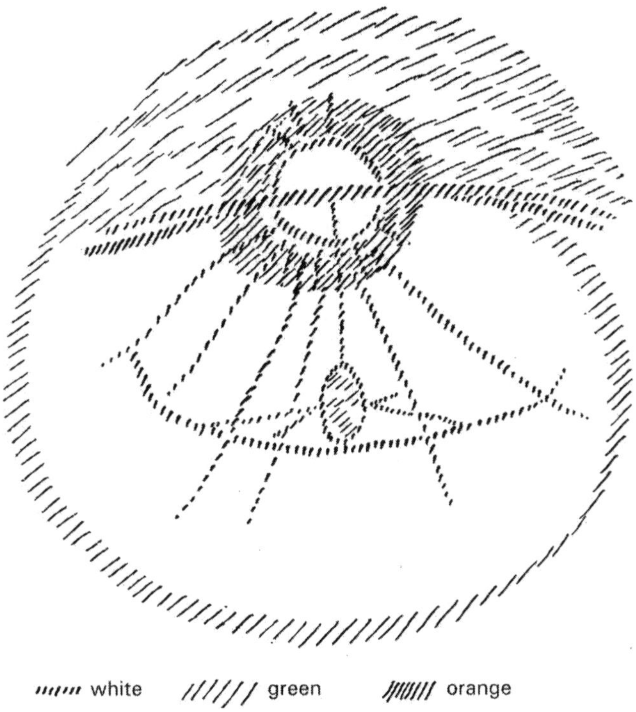

this physical body. Just as we are physically more than just our outward, delimited physical body in terms of the fact that we can bring forth a new human being from ourselves, thus going beyond ourselves in physical terms, so we are also more than ourselves in a spiritual direction. At a time of instinctive clairvoyance people knew this, and this was why saints were depicted with a halo. Just as we go beyond our own being in the physical world because we can reproduce, through the higher sun we can go beyond our ordinary soul powers, bound up with the body: we can extend further into the spirit and therefore, in the view of older times, bear a halo. When later artists depict a halo, it always looks like a cap plonked on the figure's head because they have no inkling as to how this is really connected with the human being. The halo is not a hood but something a person has through the higher sun—an expansion of his soul into spirit, to the point where this expansion becomes visible in the etheric.

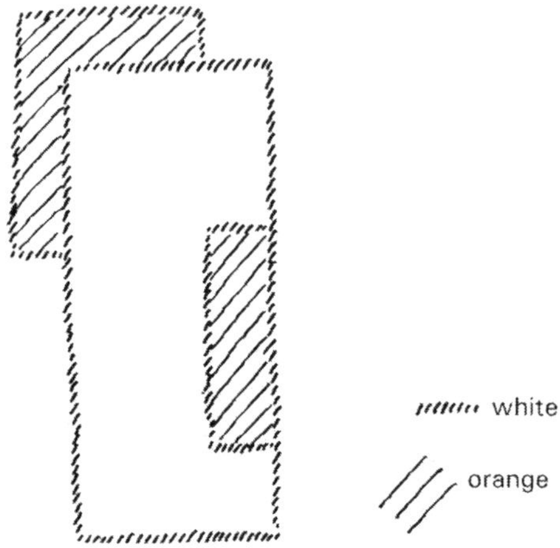

As we learn through anthroposophy to understand once again why an ancient atavistic vision endowed people with a halo, we are led deeply into the nature of soul and spirit on the one hand, and on the other into what ancient clairvoyant perceptions, albeit of a dreamlike kind, were able to observe in the world. They could perceive truths, realities. And it is uncommonly foolish of modern people to think that depictions of saints with halos in past times were mere fantasy. It was not fantasy, but to indicate that such people were primarily influenced by the higher sun, by what exists in the sun as spirit-soul. When we study the human soul, therefore, we find that it does really fill our organism; but as moon nature penetrates us, and can only manifest as reflection, we are estranged from our own physical nature. This passes into heredity. On the other hand, as the sun in turn acquires through the higher sun what it loses for the earth through the moon, we can participate in this, can reach up with our soul into the spirit already in our etheric body.

We need to describe these things if we are to show how intimately the human soul is connected with world evolution. We cannot speak of the human soul at all without speaking at the same time of world evolution. The moment we reach true soul nature we also reach sun nature. And just as we are strongly bound up with matter by virtue of the fact that we bear inherited characteristics, that we therefore embody the impulses of physical evolution, so we are bound up with the world of spirit by virtue of the fact that mere head spirituality, which actually has a somewhat corpselike, dead quality, is penetrated by higher sun nature so that this head spirituality is permeated with soul. Soul nature reaches up into our thinking. Mr Smith's courageous feelings, if he is a brave fellow, extend into and inform the idea of the lion, which is a picture in the spirit, whereas cowardly Jones's feelings make him want to take flight. In both cases the thought becomes soulful through what rises from the human organism—for what surges up into thinking can be traced back to the simmering and bubbling of the organism. In the same way, rather than drives, desires and passions, cosmic soul streams in instead from the sphere of the higher sun.

And we have to be clear that living in spiritual pictures, in thoughts, there streams into these thoughts our animal, desire nature from one direction, thus ensouling a thinking otherwise cold and prosaic [see drawing, red], while from the other direction higher sun nature streams in [yellow]—this is also soul quality. It is prejudice to believe that someone who does not simply live in emotions but can also assimilate higher sun nature from the world into his abstract

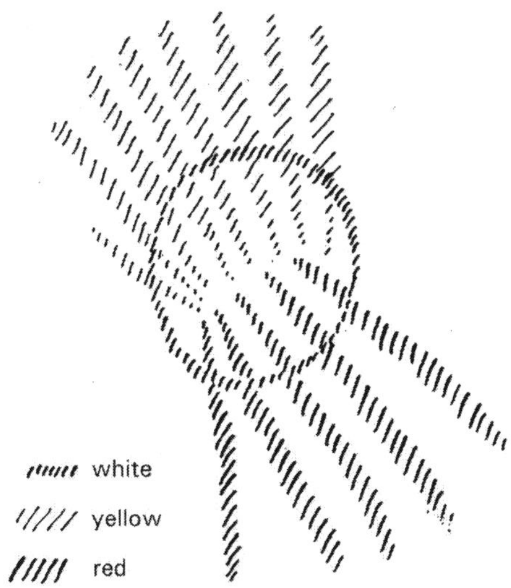

thoughts will therefore become as arid a fellow as those who only live in thoughts.

People fear spirituality when it manifests in a pure, cosmic form, because they think that they are already cold enough in their thoughts. If they absorb cosmic thoughts as well, they think, they will become stiff as old boots. But actually the reverse is true. We become just as inwardly warm—but now in a purely spiritual form—as we are when enthused by drives, desires, animal nature in us that streams up from our organism into our thought nature.

In my book *Goethe's World View*,[11] I suggested that one cannot simply warm and enliven thought by mingling it with impulse and desire. Certainly, passion and impulse make thoughts warm, but in an animal kind of way. There is also a warmth that originates in the world that comes from the higher sun. We can glow with warmth if we absorb this cosmic, rather than animal warmth, which is that of the hierarchies above the human being. I hinted at this at least in the book I refer to, speaking of how wrong it is to see someone who is full of ideas pervaded by higher warmth as a dry and arid fellow, and wrong to think that we ourselves will become so if we absorb such ideas; for they are different in quality from the dry, prosaic ideas which are the only kind most people are aware of today.

I have been attempting to describe the soul to you in its relationship with world evolution. And tomorrow we will look at particular details of this soul life.

LECTURE 5

7 MAY 1922

NATURALLY there would still be an enormous amount to say about our theme, but one can only give isolated hints and suggestions, and these will have to suffice for now. Today, in a kind of more comprehensive survey, I will try to show you how the soul is integrated into the whole of world evolution.

As ensouled human beings between birth and death, when we let our surroundings work upon us we first receive from this environment a sum of impressions. For centuries now, modern people have become accustomed through scientific education—which finds its way right down into primary schools—to seeing this outer environment as the thing of chief importance. In modern times, in fact, people have begun to construct the science of the psyche—psychology—as a kind of natural science. This is true not only of academics, but basically also of everyone, however ordinary. This is also due to modern people's reluctance, or lack of capacity, for self-reflection, and therefore they do not easily attend to things such as those we discussed yesterday. A modern person has little inclination, is little accustomed, to looking back upon himself in an objective fashion. He does attend to what I described yesterday as the upsurge and rampancy of impulses, desires, passions and emotions. But he is little inclined to observe all this objectively since in such self-reflection he discerns nothing much other than these kinds of impulses. Even if sometimes refined through education, these rising desires retain the same quality, whereas people do and can form certain ideas about their external surroundings in which they are not directly, personally involved, and which therefore have a certain objectivity.

There are many people who are not keen about such concepts and prefer to cultivate what lives in their inner subjectivity. But everywhere modern civilization is presenting them with ideas about nature such as those current today, and in fact for several centuries now. Modern people therefore fill their inner life with these ideas of natural science. Through their local newspaper and its Sunday supplement, for instance, they already learn to regard the world as dictated by this outlook. They are unaware that they are meeting a scientific worldview here, even in their little local press; but that is the case. This is ubiquitous, and so modern people concern themselves really only with concepts about external nature. I do not mean this as criticism of anyone in particular but as criticism of our time in general, or rather just by way of characterization since there is nothing to criticize here. This has arisen by necessity as the character of our age. People are so little interested in human qualities as such that they have become indifferent to whether they see a living actor on the stage or his ghost, as it were, in the cinema. In reality of course, there is a considerable difference between the two, but there is little real or deep awareness of the difference—for otherwise people would have more of a sense of how phenomena such as cinema culture are contributing in a major way to the decline of our civilization.

The ideas conveyed to a modern person's soul are ones he simply absorbs blindly on the seemingly sacrosanct authority of science. But we must be clear what it means to accept things in this way as science describes them. We actually do not know, when accepting such things on authority, what in fact occurs in science labs and so forth. Thus a blind belief in authority holds sway in relation to ideas conveyed to people about the external world.

But this has by no means always been so. I have often pointed out that in studying the history of human evolution we can discover ancient times when an instinctive, dreamlike clairvoyance, as I have always called it, existed in human beings. This clairvoyance was instinctive and dreamlike, and yet well suited to penetrating deeper into the real nature of things than today's scientific ideas. Through these ancient ideas and pictures which people today regard as merely symbolic or allegorical, or as the products of fantasy, it was indeed possible to enter reality. It mattered little whether a particular picture or legend exactly corresponded to an objective fact. By dwelling in reality with a picture, one was living vividly within a realm of spirit, whereas today, of course, the important thing is whether an idea one forms precisely corresponds with something outside us, for only through such concordance or agreement can people orientate themselves.

If we understand this, then we will have to face up squarely to something that is enormously important for evaluating the whole nature of our modern civilization. We will have to acknowledge that ancient people with their instinctive clairvoyance had something alive in their soul, which modern people say is only fantasy and simply does not accord with the external facts.

When we stand on an anthroposophic foundation with real understanding we must in a sense go along with this faithful reflection of the world, in which we are no longer actually within external nature but only create a reflection or image of it. You may know that we embrace the scientific method entirely inasmuch as we reject every type of hypothesis about natural phenomena, and instead, in our phenomenalism, as we must call it, remain within phenomena themselves—that is, within external natural phenomena that must explain themselves, to cite Goethe.[12] In other words we do not add to these phenomena hypotheses about atoms and their bombardments, explosions and so forth, as is still current today due to the sluggishness of old habits of thinking. On anthroposophic foundations we have to keep faith to the strictest degree with the outward phenomena of nature, and reject an approach that projects ideas onto these phenomena.

We can best learn how to avoid such projections if we adhere to something that also emerged with the scientific world-view in humanity's recent evolution—that is, technology. If we make technical and technological use of natural laws, we ourselves are really creating the phenomena. Of course, there will always be an intrinsic force within the phenomena, say the power of electricity, which modern scientists will tell you is something they use but whose nature they do not fully understand. Scientists will frequently say this of all natural forces, also heat, light and so on. Residues of this outlook remain. But what really counts in technology we seek to master is what we ourselves combine in experiments, so that we have a certain insight into what is happening.

Someone aware of these things can have the following experience. In the technology he constructs, or also in the field of chemical technology, lies something of a direct, comprehensible certainty; whereas in speaking of our observations of nature there is potential for disagreement and diverse ways of thinking. We can therefore say that modern thinking is really most perfectly embodied in the engineer. Someone today who is devoid of understanding about how a machine is built or, let's say, how a chemical preparation is made, and how they are used, is not yet thinking in tune with his times. We can say that he is allowing others to think within him, since really innovative people are engaging in technological thinking. And so the modern world-view has gradually become what we find realized in technology, mechanics, chemistry and so on. This has gradually expanded to encompass the only way of considering the world that is thought valid.

What is our astronomy really? For a long time it was nothing other than an account of the cosmic mechanism. People pictured a great machine involving movements of the sun and the planets. Chemism has now been added in the form of spectral analysis.[13] But astronomy gets no further than this. This science of the cosmos today only really answers the question as to how we best form an idea of the cosmos if we simply project onto it what we are able to observe in technology. In other words, today our science only has really valid ideas—with the exception of what one is tempted to call pure drivel such as neovitalism,[14] or nonsense about psychoids[15] and suchlike—

in so far as we can create and construct machines and chemical preparations. The ideas we gain from these acts of construction we then project onto the structure of the cosmos, picturing it to ourselves as a great machine within which certain types of chemical process are at work.

It was not always thus. Until well into the fifteenth century—I am speaking here of regions at the forefront of civilization—people still dwelt in ideas about the external universe that were not purely technological but instead engendered an experience in them. Technology is something entirely outside us, detached from us. People once engaged more nearly with what they knew, and experienced it more closely. This is why very clever, modern minds always have a feeling that in olden times people dreamed their knowledge, projecting all kinds of things onto the world—lived in fantasies. Only today are we able to picture the world without such colouring of the imagination. And people think now that technical ideas are the only ones we should allow ourselves to project on the world, and we will then avoid the danger of fantasizing about it and failing to recognize its true nature.

But there is something much, much deeper underlying what I am describing—something that the prophets of the ancient mysteries emphasized at a certain level or degree of initiation. In the days when ancient clairvoyance existed, adepts of the mysteries had prophetic vision of the world-view that would one day emerge. This vision showed them, roughly, that if the world-view that held sway in those early times, when people experienced their surroundings in an instinctive, dreamlike way, were to be retained the human being could never become free. This inner experience of the world would always dictate the impulses of their actions too. A divine world would dawn in their hearts, said these prophets, but this divine world would make them unfree. Ancient civilizations were indeed peopled by an unfree humankind. They knew that what they did, except where this was imposed by state laws and rulers, hearkened to divine commands. In other words, they fulfilled and performed the dictates of divine impulses.

In the mysteries it was said that a time must come when this kind of divine working ceases in people, when, instead, they will only look outwards into their external surroundings, finding there things that no longer have any human connection, and absorbing this outer world into their souls. When human beings can no longer perceive and experience intrinsically human powers but only forces that dwell in the external world, which have no intimate connection with them, then they will be inwardly free, inwardly unburdened; and then their soul will be filled only with things that do not concern their own organization.

This phase of evolution has to come, a time when people will focus their gaze on nature outside them so that they can become free. That is what people said in the ancient mysteries; and therefore they acknowledged that one day they would no longer be able to give what they still could at that time to those who approached them with understanding. They predicted the emergence of a science that instigates no impulses in people but does supply them with ideas of what is outside them. They saw that the knowledge and perception of future times would in this way be focused always only on the external world, allowing people by contrast to educate their inner impulses towards freedom.

It was this fact, you see, that was so very present in my mind when I felt an intense prompting to write first my preparatory books and then *The Philosophy of Freedom.*[16] The following was the fundamental issue in writing this book: to say with all clarity that we are now in the age of technology; and other than perpetuating the old with little awareness, preserving what is contained in traditional confessions and so forth of the world-views of former, instinctive times, our only option is to orient ourselves to technological ideas about the world, to mechanistic ideas. The world we now inhabit is regarded as a great machine and a chemistic complex. If we are to return to the spirit, you see, we must break radically with all the old mysticism of former times, instead finding the spirit in what one might call the spirit-less, mechanical world that modern science has given us.

I would like to draw a schematic picture of this situation we faced as I was writing my *Philosophy of Freedom*. If this is the human being [drawing, left, white] and this is our environment [yellow], then in former times we should picture things like this. The human being looked out into his surroundings, and also experienced within him what was given him by his instinctive, dreamlike clairvoyance [red]. He united this with what he saw in his surroundings, and this is why he saw them as imbued with spirit [red in yellow]. In all creatures he saw elemental or also higher beings by virtue of the inner state with which he met them.

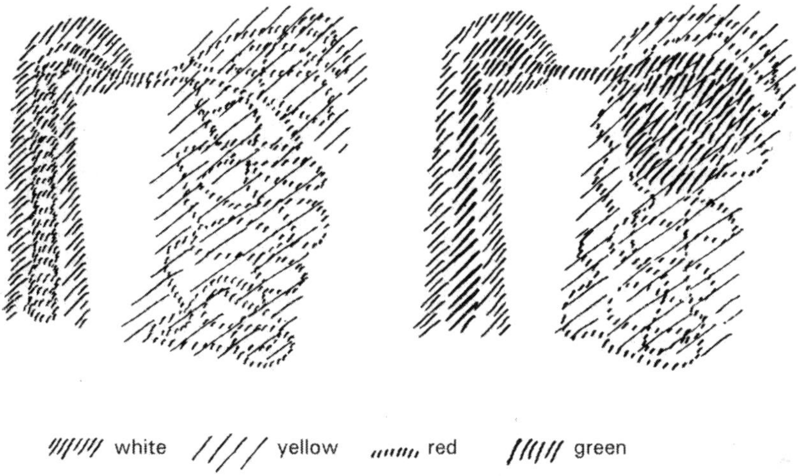

Here by contrast [drawing, right, white] is a modern human being in contemporary culture, for whom, really, I wrote my *Philosophy of Freedom* at the end of the 1880s and beginning of the 90s; and here are his surroundings [yellow]. Now people no longer bring forth something from within them and infuse their surroundings with it, but they only trace there what can be constructed as technology: they trace there the laws of these surroundings themselves. But no moral impulse can be derived from this—only natural laws can be formulated by this means. As I have drawn this here [left], people in ancient times were still one with the world and therefore could perceive moral impulses in everything they saw, in stones, animals, plants; and this is because all these things contained divine, spiritual beings. There is nothing left of this in our natural laws, which only offer what can be incorporated into machines or mechanisms.

What therefore was the task I needed to undertake with this book, *The Philosophy of Freedom*? It was this. If we can no longer find any moral impulses outside us in nature, since we only access the realm of natural laws through our sense perceptions, then we must emerge and go forth from ourselves, we can no longer remain inside ourselves. And therefore I had to describe this initial emergence in which we depart from our corporeality—and this occurs in pure thinking, as I showed in the book. This means that we no longer go out of ourselves with an instinctive clairvoyance, but instead depart from our body altogether and place ourselves out there in our surroundings [green]. And what does this give us? Here, in accomplishing a very first, and most subtle clairvoyance, we discover moral intuitions; or, if you wish to use the more subjective expression I used back then, a faculty of moral imagination. We depart from ourselves in this process, discovering in the realm of technology—in which the spirit is therefore still present—a spiritual aspect in this first domain, in the domain of morality.

But people failed to see that I was describing here the first stage of a modern clairvoyance. They held fast to the idea that clairvoyance is something that plunges us into unclarity, where we enter a vague and unknown realm. In fact I was describing how to seek what can be known through emerging from ourselves in thinking that now no longer adheres to materiality but grasps itself in itself, since the world can here be grasped in pure—in fact the purest—spirituality.

And this is why *The Philosophy of Freedom* was destined to seem too intellectual to mystics. They saw it as containing too much thinking, while the others, the rationalists and scientists, or also modern philosophers, could make nothing of it because it led into the realm of vision which they did not wish to enter. They wished to stay with merely outward observation, even if they were speaking philosophically. And yet the whole stance and gesture of *The Philosophy of Freedom* was a fulfilment of the task facing modern humankind.

This is what can be said, in an elementary way, about the prophetic vision of ancient initiates in the mysteries. However, they actually saw things in a rather more detailed way—they saw a connection here with the human soul and with world evolution, which we can express as follows. Yes, the world that later knowledge will discover is in fact not just external to humankind but also external to the gods, is outside the sphere of divine creation of which these initiates spoke. They sought revelation of the divine in what they achieved through their initiation, and by means of this they communicated with divine beings. The diverse pre-Christian peoples consorted with 'their' divine beings—the Hebrew people, for instance, with their Yahweh or Jehovah. In so far as they were initiates, they not only communicated in thoughts but in reality. It is correct to speak of real communication with these divine beings in the ancient mysteries. Yes, initiates consorted with these divine beings; but when they were not within the mysteries and when their pupils were not, they all saw their surroundings once again. However they saw this outer world in a way that involved placing into it from within them what their instinctive clairvoyance endowed them with. But the initiates themselves, particularly, and their pupils, knew that their external environment in a way resisted what their vision informed it with; and they knew too that a time would come when it would no longer just offer resistance but when human perception would see there only what it can perceive without such 'informing' from within.

The ancient initiates acknowledged a truth that modern people do not have the courage to because their knowledge is too superficial, insufficiently profound. They said that if they did not inform the world they saw around them with what the gods had given them—which they had been endowed with at the beginning of world evolution—then the world would be empty of the gods. In other words, they acknowledged an external world that does not originate with the gods with whom they consorted in the mysteries.

It is this outlook that lived on in the Middle Ages in a particular form of asceticism and disdain for the world of nature. It lives on still today in certain confessions, albeit in a very dissembling manner.

Originating in the ancient mysteries, this outlook is that by gazing inwards I can communicate with gods, but the outer world around me has not been created at all by the gods I seek to find by my intense efforts when I undergo initiation.

This was a basic insight which people increasingly accepted as a mundane truth—that the outer world does not originate with the gods people had come to know through the mysteries and initiation. These gods actually desired a quite different world. Through a particular event, the human being sank down into this world which his gods had not in the least wanted. All ideas about the Fall—we could digress here and examine them all, but we don't have the time—originate in the human perception that the world we know as our outer surroundings is not the one the gods created.

But people sought to grasp what these gods, with whom they consorted, wished now to accomplish in relation to this world. It was possible to learn this from them. The lesson imparted was that they really desired that this world be pulverized, destroyed.

The initiates of ancient times faced this fact: that the gods towards whom they strove revealed to humankind their resolve to destroy this world. And yet the initiates also knew that to become free eventually human beings must connect their knowledge and perception with this world which the gods consider ripe for destruction.

In the older Greek mysteries this was understood in a very unique way. In the most ancient Greek mysteries, in particular, people were working towards an artistic shaping of the world. In ancient Greece there was no inkling of a scientific world-view such as we have today. In sculpture, especially also in dramatic tragedy, and in art in general, efforts were being made to create something through human endeavour which does relate to this world and yet also goes beyond it. The Greek initiate thought that this earth on which he stood, the world of trees that he saw, of springs that he perceived and so forth, will disappear into dust. But what of this world has been mysteriously infused into the figure of Venus of Milo, Zeus, Athene or the dramas of Sophocles will, it is true, pass from the visible realm into the invisible, but these thoughts will remain hovering there as it were, and when the earth returns to dust they will go forth and redeem the future of the earth which otherwise could only come to an end in this world's radical destruction.

As long as art still issued from the mysteries, the most ancient Greeks believed that they would be able to save from decline and destruction the world that originated with the gods, but which these gods themselves had resolved to destroy. This knowledge led people to say the following. You see, certain fundamental scientific realities were already known to ancient initiates, as can be historically proven. Of course we have added a great deal more knowledge in the course of recent centuries, especially the nineteenth, in relation to technical construction. Yet certain fundamental things that still play their part today in technology were certainly known to ancient initiates. They knew a great deal more than they told those who were not initiated. But they said the following to themselves. If we simply combine natural forces to create something mechanical, in an extreme scenario we will have something that will go under with the earth, whose destruction the gods themselves desire. You see, every initiate knows that the gods to whom people looked up in the ancient mysteries, with whom they consorted in the mysteries, and with whom of course we can still communicate today, hate nothing so much as, say, a train or a car. These are terrible things for them. It is the view of these gods that what they had to put up with from Ahriman when he formed the earth in this mechanical way is now being copied by humankind. Human beings add to his works. The gods consider that they already have enough to do to destroy the works of Ahriman, but in addition to this they must now deal with these steam engines, these electrical machines and all such things. They too will have to be destroyed.

And so the old initiates said to themselves: 'It will do no good at all if, in technical machines or technical chemism, we simply multiply external powers of nature that are no longer informed by spiritual vision.' These initiates were fundamentally persuaded that this was so. Instead they thought they must save as much of this world as they could. As I said, in ancient Greece they wished to save it through art.

Further towards the Orient, people believed that what runs merely in accordance with the so-called laws of nature basically has no purpose at all for humanity's true evolution, for the gods will eventually blast it to smithereens. Therefore they sought to act in a way that would allow spirit to indwell it, and this gave rise to ancient forms of worship—not the creation of machinery or chemism, but ritual acts of worship. In what one does one sees something sacred or sacramental, something that contains spirituality, in which the spirit is also at work. In religious worship people thus sought to save as much as it is possible to save of earthly evolution.

On previous occasions I have often used a picture to express this, that of the altar which our laboratory table should become[17] so that we move beyond mere technology: so that we do in fact undertake a kind of divine service when we work in the physics or chemistry lab. The laboratory table can become an altar for our moral, spiritual activity. This picture I offered previously is basically the same thing as I have been saying today from a more historical perspective.

Thus arose the religious worship to which people today are returning because they cannot find the resources to become spiritually active. It is remarkable that intelligent people, in particular, are today returning in large numbers to the bosom of the Catholic Church, simply because they wish to take refuge in what will remain of the earth after everything else has vanished entirely through the will of the gods themselves. Those who do not observe modern life attentively completely overlook this stream of educated people, especially, into the arms of Catholicism. The latter seek to flee the destruction that will come by taking refuge in something which, like the Catholic ceremonies and rituals that derive from very ancient traditions, can give form at least to what survives. And they seek refuge in this way because they lack the activity that can find something really new, something that we need for the future. People lack this inner strength, which they have lost in the course of our technological age.

At a certain moment people would have needed to acknowledge, in energetic fashion, that they now stand within the negative world of technology in which impulses of the older kind can no longer be found, and that therefore they should take the step towards moral imagination, to Intuition. That is what they should have said. But those who overlook this need of our time return to Catholicism. This is understandable, given the frailty of our time.

These realities, and the perception of them by ancient initiates, led them to ask how things would develop since the gods of whom they knew, and with whom they consorted through the mysteries, sought the earth's destruction. They were aware of this contradiction: that if people were to become free they would increasingly develop an affinity with what exists on earth, for only through the advent of technical knowledge can they gain freedom. If this had been their only insight, the old initiates would have faced the terrible future prospect, revealed to their prophetic vision, of a future state of affairs in which, to become fully human, people would have to become completely entangled in the godless ahrimanic world, and thus be pulverized along with the earth when the gods dissolve it. In this view, people will themselves increasingly become machines, come to resemble machines, their thoughts subsumed entirely in technical impulses. Astronomy is now basically nothing other than thoughts about the great cosmic machinery. Human thoughts are filled with mechanical thinking. You see ultimately it is all the same whether we think about screws and cogwheels or about Venus and Mercury in a model constructed along the same, purely technological lines.

These initiates would have faced this terrible prospect. And it was clear to them that their old gods sought this destruction because, inevitably, they sought the destruction of the ahrimanic element and, as things stood at first, they could not save humankind.

But in these ancient mysteries this was in turn balanced by another prophetic vision, of the future Mystery of Golgotha. After this event had occurred, people increasingly became able to grasp it in some way or other. But prophetically the old initiates learned of this event from the gods with whom they consorted. The gods knew all; and all-encompassing wisdom could be gained from them. But there was one thing that could never be learned from them—matters relating to human birth and death. The gods knew nothing, especially, of death as such. Yet in these ancient mysteries it was known that one from the ranks of the gods was to be sent down to earth, the one who was later called Christ, and would come to know death upon earth. The Mystery of Golgotha lies in this: that one of the gods who formerly did not know death, nor therefore birth or all the conditions of heredity, came to know death. By virtue of this, he connected with earthly evolution and could thus offer a counterbalance to what would inevitably have occurred through our evolution towards freedom—our ever-increasing affinity with the pulverizing earth. We ourselves can create this counter-pole if, on the one hand, we really do dedicate ourselves to modern knowledge, modern scientific insights, but on the other turn towards Christ, one of the gods, who came to know death, and thus also birth.

On the one hand, therefore, we can incline fully to what is necessary for our freedom, but on the other—on, if you like, the other pan of the scales—we can find our way to the Pauline phrase 'Not I but Christ in me'. And then, by permeating the world with Christ, we will again find the means from within us to reshape, reconfigure what must otherwise lapse from the divine world to which we intrinsically belong.

And thus Christ was set against the ahrimanic powers who act on earth in what would otherwise have lapsed. Through a resolve of the super-earthly gods, Christ was set against these powers and now works on within the earthly realm. He has no need to become free, for he is a god and remains so in passing through death. He does not become similar to earth but lives as god within the earth. And this means that we now have, on the one hand, the ability to place as much as possible on the freedom side of the scales, really to pursue individualism to its ultimate consequences—for it is only in the individual human being that moral imagination will be found . This is why my *Philosophy of Freedom* has been called the most extreme individualism. It had to be this, since it is, on the other hand, the most Christian of philosophies. On the one side of the scales had to be placed natural science, knowledge of the natural world in the fullest sense, which we only penetrate through the spirit, by raising ourselves to pure, free thinking. This can still be saved, redeemed within purely technological knowledge. On the other side of the scales, though, we must place true knowledge of Christ, which is at the same time true knowledge of the Mystery of Golgotha.

It was therefore self-evident that I had to try to write *The Philosophy of Freedom*, naturally with its inevitable flaws since one cannot do everything perfectly at the first attempt. But on the other hand, in my books *Eleven European Mystics* and *Christianity as Mystical Fact*,[18] it was necessary for me to point to the Mystery of Golgotha. These two things simply belong together. Those who find this contradictory think I'm putting two ridiculously different things on the scales—meat on one side and weights on the other, say—whereas in fact the two belong together. If you take the weights away and add them to the meat, there will of course be no balance any more. Modern critics do something like this: they place mysticism on one side and philosophy on the other, and then muddle the two together—and then think that the world is badly misbehaving. And yet to confuse things in this way is to exclude everything needed in our era. If modern souls are to find the right orientation to world evolution, they must develop a strong impulse for freedom on the one hand, and on the other an equally strong impulse for inner experience of the Mystery of Golgotha.

In both science, and in the life of individuals, this is something that must emerge and develop further. Humankind, each individual, must eventually overcome old, instinctive forms of mysticism and place themselves entirely on the footing of the kind of knowledge we have, say, when we understand a steam engine. My *Philosophy of Freedom* was founded only on such ideas of external science—the kind of thinking needed to understand a steam engine. But to do this, though we lay aside our whole being, we do not dispense with its ultimate capacity, that of pure thinking. This must still be developed in humankind, and then applied. But this is at the same time what lives within outward objects.

So we can place ourselves entirely on the footing of freedom, yet equally, at the same time, on the ground of the reality of Christ. And this must also penetrate science. It will do so by our contemplating external nature, describing it, if you like in Haeckel's[19] terms—which leaves residues that can never be understood through such ideas. Forgive me if I speak rather plainly here, but we are, aren't we, serious folk who really do seek understanding, and not just a little edifying teatime chatter? Two things are needed, must enter our civilization in the right way; and these things informed the depiction of the halo in past eras, in which people knew through their instinctive clairvoyance that we are connected with a spiritual environment. In these most ancient times, the halo was very especially developed, and appears in the most diverse forms, also in acts and rites of worship. But as the first signs of materialism awoke in people's feelings in medieval times, another image began to come to the fore: the pregnant woman. Look at these medieval paintings—all the women in them are pregnant. Here we see on the one hand what is saved, redeemed from death, expressed in its highest form in the annunciation of the world of spirit in the halo; and on the other we see birth, which repeatedly brings human beings into the physical world.

All these things are connected with the inner, spiritual engine of our evolution. The soul always lives in such inner, evolutionary impulses. There is a connection, therefore, between the most intimate facts of soul experience and world evolution itself; and science will also gradually have to accommodate itself to this, and acknowledge that a rigorous view of the world based on Haeckel will leave out two things, one of which is birth and the other death. These cannot be grasped through ideas originating in chemistry and mechanics, or from what can be constructed technically. These two gateways lead us forth from such ideas, and here a different mode of thought and observation is needed. As long as we are concerned with freedom we can stay within ideas that manifest in technology. And if someone writes a *Philosophy of Freedom*, this is not for children, who are not yet free, for the divine still works in them in unfreedom, but for people in their adult years, for only then do we actually become free. And if this person goes on to write the other works I have done, we are led directly to a view we can entertain in our souls about death. In the very first chapters of my mystical writings,[20] therefore, you can find the primal mystery of the experience of death, and an inner experience of death and spiritual rebirth.

This is something that simply emerges by itself from a contemporary observation of the world—not in some nebulous way, but by thoroughly grasping what is really necessary today. We have to acknowledge that the human soul's experience of freedom brings it in touch with the ahrimanic element. And what it experiences in religious inclination, even if this leads towards the Mystery of Golgotha, comes very close to the luciferic. And then it is very easy, if we only develop egoistical religious instincts, as often happens in religion nowadays, for us also to succumb to luciferic drives and instincts.

The modern world is asking us to take account of this in relation to the soul; and this is also what Christ taught his intimate disciples immediately after his Resurrection. These intimate pupils, who carried on the old mystery initiation, were to teach that Christ descended from the world of gods as yet ignorant of death, and who therefore could not tell the earliest human beings anything about death. These disciples were to teach that Christ descended to learn of the secrets of birth and death. This is also why teachings about Christ's own birth and death remained so unclear—because people did not find ways to explain these things. But in the founding Christian mysteries, whose meaning was lost as early as the fourth century AD since the sense of freedom first had to be developed, Christ himself, after his Resurrection, taught his first initiated pupils this secret of a god becoming acquainted with earthly death. But this occurred after the old gods had imparted to human beings the old, primordial wisdom, which was passed on through one generation after another, becoming ever more dilute. What Christ imparted to his intimate disciples after his Resurrection was the most intrinsic, primary revelation about earthly life, a spiritual foundation that was to sustain the life of the soul in the further course of evolution. Basically, you see, what the old gods taught human beings who raised themselves to them in the mysteries were the secrets of Saturn, Sun, Moon. The intrinsic secret of the earth—only on the earth did birth and death first arise as human beings know it; previously there was only metamorphosis, transformation—first had to be experienced by a God who became acquainted with death on earth through the Mystery of Golgotha in order to impart this revelation to the life of the human soul. This most fundamental revelation after Christ's death thus also created the foundation the human soul must assimilate in order to accomplish the redemption of earthly life.

Thus human souls are connected with the evolution of the earth, with the evolution of the world altogether. They are connected with it also by virtue of the other things I have described over the past days. They are connected with it when they rightly take up the impulse of the Mystery of Golgotha, as I wished to show in these lectures.

Part Two

SPIRITUAL STRIVING IN RELATION TO THE EARTH'S EVOLUTION

Lecture 6

26 MAY 1922

We have often described here the child's early stages of development. Many years ago,[21] I drew attention to the fact that up to the second dentition a child is primarily an imitative being. He strongly, and in a sense instinctively, experiences within him everything that occurs around him in the same way that at a later stage of life he experiences, subliminally, what happens around him only through his sense organs.

In our eyes, in fact, we have a process that to some degree imitates what happens outside us, just as a camera imitates what is outside it. We experience this imitation of the world in our eyes, and thereby gain our knowledge of the outer world. The same is true of our other senses. This imitative principle only becomes confined, if you like, to the human periphery at a later age. In the child up to the second dentition the whole body, albeit to a lesser degree, is involved in this imitation. Here we can say that the whole body relates to the child's surroundings as later only the senses do. He is primarily an imitative being, whose inner nature orients itself to his environment and the effect of this outer world upon him as he imitates it. This is why it is so important that at this age we do nothing in the child's proximity that the child cannot absorb and assimilate—and this includes the very way we think and feel.

At second dentition it becomes possible for the child to respond to the world not just like a sense organ but to assimilate thoughts and ideas. The child begins—and increasingly develops this ability—to take what we say as a guideline for his actions, whereas previously our guideline for him was everything we did in his proximity. He can now encompass what we say to him. This is why the adult becomes an authority figure for the child between second dentition and puberty. It is important for the child to hearken, and to orient himself, in a self-evident way to what we say to him. Language itself is learned through imitation, but only from second dentition does the child assign decisive importance to what can be expressed in language, and what the adult can therefore tell the child. And the actual critical faculty, where a young lady or gentleman, as we must now say, begins to exercise their power of judgement, only starts from puberty. Only then can we assume that the adolescent begins to form his own views from within.

Well, this is an initial outward characterization of things, a way of describing how the child grows into the world, as we can always discover through unprejudiced observation. All this is connected with remarkable inner processes; and it is of these that I wish to speak today. Hitherto I have always stated that the human etheric body lives in intimate connection with the physical body up to the time when second dentition begins to occur. This is why I said that we can regard the change of teeth as the real birth of the human etheric body. Similarly we can speak of the real birth of the astral body at puberty. But these are only outward characterizations, and today we will consider these things from a somewhat more inward perspective.

If we observe the human being long before he develops an inclination to descend to physical embodiment, we find him to be a spirit-soul in an environment of spirit and soul. All of us were in this condition before we descended to unite with the physical body prepared in our mother's womb. We unite with this physical body to pass through our earthly existence between birth and death. For a long period prior to this, as I said, we were beings of spirit and soul in a world of spirit and soul. What we are there, and what we experience too, is greatly different from what we experience here on earth between birth and death. This is why it is so difficult to describe experiences between death and rebirth—because they are so very different from earthly conditions. Our ideas develop according to earthly experiences and are informed by them, and we are always reliant on these ideas. Tomorrow and the next day we will give further consideration to our existence in the world of spirit and soul itself, but today we will turn to the time when we are approaching a new descent to earth with a view to permeating ourselves with a physical body.

What first happens before we approach our physical body, the embryo, the germ of our physical body, is that we draw towards us forces from the etheric world. Here on earth we live in the physical world: the world characterized by everything we can perceive through our senses and grasp through our earthly reason. But there is nothing in this world that is not also pervaded by the etheric world. This physical world we see, hear and so forth, is everywhere infused with the etheric world, and we first live our way towards this world before approaching the physical world. Before we gain the inclination and impetus to unite with the physical world through the embryo, we draw towards us forces of the etheric world, forming and developing our ether body by doing so.

In order to absorb these ideas more precisely, let us draw them schematically on the board. This form here depicts the spirit and soul approaching from the world of spirit [drawing, p. 90, violet; the drawing is gradually completed as Steiner gives the following account]. Of course this is completely schematic. Only what we first draw towards us in this way becomes our etheric body. In other words, we can say that we cloak ourselves with our etheric body [orange shading] as we descend from the world of spirit. But saying that we 'cloak ourselves with our etheric body' does not tell us a great deal. We have to study the properties of this etheric body in a little more detail. This etheric body developing in us is a kind of world in itself, though it is more accurate to say a 'world in itself as image'. For instance, the periphery of this etheric body reveals something starlike [yellow stars] while its lower portion displays something that

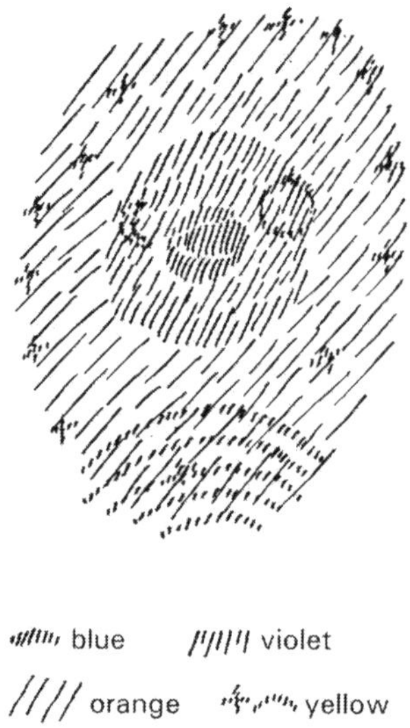

appears more or less like an image of the earth. Indeed, it even contains a kind of image or reflection of sun and moon qualities.

It is extraordinarily significant that, as we draw etheric forces towards us during our descent into the earthly world, we take with us a kind of image of the cosmos. If we could isolate the human etheric body at the moment when we unite with the physical body, we would find a sphere with stars, the zodiac, sun and moon—far lovelier than anything ever constructed in a mechanical model.

These configurations of the etheric body are still present as we grow increasingly one with our physical body during the period of embryonic development, although they grow paler. They continue to be present until the child is seven or eight, until the second dentition. This cosmic sphere can still be discerned in the child's ether body. When the second dentition begins around seven, the forms we can discern in the etheric body start to radiate, we can say. I will draw this schematically for the period, roughly, between seven and fourteen, from the change of teeth to puberty {see drawing on p. 91, red rays}. As I said, these configurations grow paler during embryonic development, and continue to fade afterwards, but are still clearly present. But from the change of teeth onwards they fade entirely,

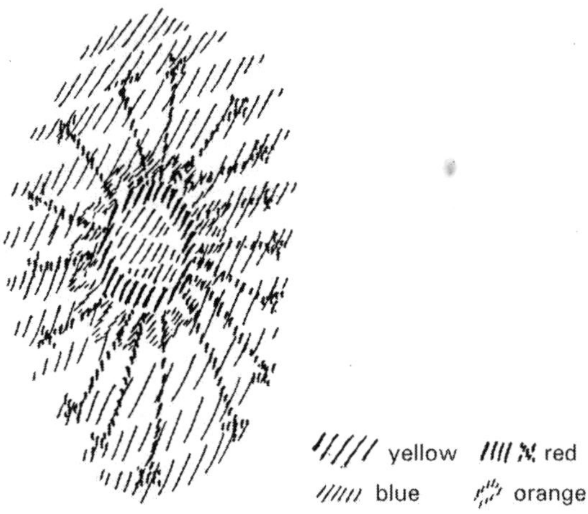

though at the same time sending rays inwards [red]. We can put it like this: the stars in the human ether body dissolve and become rays that have the tendency to meet in the interior.

All this occurs slowly and gradually during this whole period from the change of teeth to puberty. By puberty these rays have grown together here and merge in a kind of distinct form, an etheric figure [red]. The peripheral stars, we can say, first ray inwards and later this ceases and they grow completely pale. Naturally something always remains, but it fades and grows pale. These rays likewise become pale. But what has gathered and concentrated in the centre here grows especially vivid. During the period when puberty begins, the physical heart hangs as it were in what has become concentrated in this centre. So this is the place in the human organism where the physical heart and its blood vessels can be found.

The distinctive thing here is that the star ether body draws inwards. Naturally it remains available as ether body for the whole person, but is present at the human periphery, outside and around him, and is later undifferentiated so that one can perceive little difference within it. But during the period from second dentition to puberty it is very radiant from outside inwards.

And then this all condenses and concentrates, and hanging within this figure you can clearly see the physical heart. Do not imagine, please, that we don't have an ether heart before this, we do; but we acquire this in a different way from what subsequently becomes our ether heart. What gathers and concentrates from puberty onwards does indeed become our etheric heart. Until then, as I said, we also have an etheric heart, but we acquired this through heredity, as a legacy of the forces contained in the embryo. Once we have our etheric body, and bear this with us towards the physical organism, then a kind of etheric heart, a provisional one, is drawn together through the powers of the physical body. But this childhood ether heart—and the expression I will use now is not very pleasant, but it is still a very accurate term here—gradually rots. And as it rots and becomes redundant it is continuously replaced by the etheric heart which, gathering and concentrating the whole cosmic sphere, is truly a picture of the cosmos—an etheric form we bring with us as we step through conception and birth into earthly existence.

And so one can trace a clear change in the whole form and structure of the etheric body that we bear in us during the time between birth, or already from conception, up to puberty. And we can say that only at puberty is the human being's own etheric heart present, formed and developed out of his etheric body and no longer only a provisional one created by external forces.

And all the ether forces at work in us up to puberty have the tendency to provide us with this fresh etheric heart. There is a real comparison to be made here with the change of teeth. At second dentition, of course, our inherited teeth are expelled and other teeth, our own now, replace them. In the same way the inherited etheric heart we have until puberty is expelled and we acquire our own etheric heart. That is the important thing: that we receive our own etheric heart.

Parallel with this, though, something else occurs in us. If we observe a very young child who has recently entered the physical world, we can distinguish a great many separate organs within his astral body. As I have just described, we configure our etheric body as an image of the outer world. But in our astral body we bring with us a reflection of what we experienced between our previous death and latest birth. One can discern an extraordinary amount in the child's astral body—it is inscribed with great secrets. We see there a great deal of the experiences between death and the latest birth. This astral body is extraordinarily differentiated and individual. And the remarkable thing is that, at the same time as what I described for the etheric body is occurring, this strongly differentiated astral body becomes less and less differentiated. Originally it is a form which, if we study it with understanding, reveals that it originates in another world, has arrived here from a world that does not exist either in the physical or the ether world. But everything living in the astral body, in a great many separate forms, slips into our physical organs, we can say, up to the time of puberty and, in fact, if I can express this roughly—it isn't precise—only into the organs above the diaphragm. Wondrous forms that are present and radiant in the astral body in the first days of life gradually slip into the developing brain and also fill the sense organs. Then others slip into the organs of respiration, others into the heart, and through the heart into the arteries. They do not enter the stomach directly but only spread out through the arteries as far as the organs of the abdomen. But gradually we can see the whole astral body the child has brought with him into physical existence at birth immersing itself in the organs, slipping into them. And so, to coin a rather odd expression but one that arises directly from reality—though of course it will appear paradoxical compared with ordinary ideas people have of the world—by the time we have grown to adulthood our organs have 'locked up' within them the separate forms of our astral body. This more intimate knowledge of the human organs can only be comprehended if we understand the nature of the human astral body that we bring with us at birth. We have to recognize that every single organ bears a certain astral element as legacy or inheritance, just as the etheric heart is initially also inherited, but that gradually this inherited astral element is entirely pervaded by the astral body we ourselves bring with us, which slowly and surely immerses itself in our physical and etheric organs. In a way the heart is an exception; within it both the etheric and the astral processes are concentrated, and this is why the heart is such an especially important organ for the human being.

Thus the astral body becomes ever less defined because it sends its tangible forms and configurations, which it brought with it from another life through conception and birth, down into the physical organs. There they are locked up, and this means that the astral body becomes more or less always a mere cloudy, misty form.

But the most interesting thing is that though, from this perspective, the astral body becomes hazy or cloudlike, other kinds of differentiation slowly emerge from puberty onwards, and then, in a very regular fashion, increasingly become apparent.

When the young child wriggles his legs, we discern very little of this wriggling in his astral body. It does induce effects there but the differentiations the astral body brought with it are so strong that, overall, things are like this:

If I draw the astral body here, it contains wondrous forms. This is only schematic, but it is derived from reality. These configurations gradually vanish, slipping into the physical organs so that the astral body increasingly becomes a kind of undefined cloud. But as I said, when a child makes wriggling movements, all sorts of things rise from these motions into the astral body yet meet resistance from what is already there, are reflected back [red] and vanish again. It is like making an indent in a rubber ball, which immediately disappears again. However intense they are, the movements of the child's wriggling make only a passing impression in the astral body and do not remain there. Now as the child then learns to speak and develops thoughts that remain in his memory, develops the capacity for speech and memory, we see increasingly that the movements the child carries out—no longer just random motions but purposeful movements such as walking and arm movements—are no longer reflected back, but these movements remain in the astral body instead. Yes, a very great deal can be inscribed into this astral body.

If you are 45 years old, almost all movements and much else, as we will see in a moment, have inscribed their traces in the astral body. The astral body can assimilate a great deal of what has occurred since you learned to speak and think, and since the astral body dissolved its own configurations. And thus wondrous forms present in the child's astral body slowly become undifferentiated by vanishing gradually into the organs. The astral body becomes an undifferentiated configuration, not entirely of course, but relatively undifferentiated. Into this undifferentiated structure are inscribed all the movements we carry out with our arms and legs. But what we *do* with our arms and legs is also inscribed, everything we have done in the external world. For instance, if we write with a pen, chop wood, or box someone's ears, this is inscribed. Even if we do not do something ourselves but ask a servant to do it, the relationship between the content of our words and what the servant does is inscribed also. In other words, a human being's whole work and activity, in so far as this finds expression in the outer world, is inscribed in the astral body [red in yellow]. Thus the astral body is configured in the most manifold way by human action and activity.

[During the following comments, Steiner completes the board drawing above. See also drawing on page 97.]

As I said, this begins when the child learns to speak, learns to embody thoughts in language. This does not yet happen in relation to the ideas the child absorbs but which we cannot later recall, but only from the time we can ordinarily remember back to. From then on, everything we do is inscribed in the astral body.

Now the remarkable thing is that everything inscribed in this way has a tendency to converge within us, in the same way that the rays of the ether body converge in our etheric heart. All human actions also converge there. And this convergence also now has a kind of external cause. Simply by the fact of being human, we have to grow into a certain activity from childhood onwards. This activity is expressed, as I just suggested, through the whole astral body. But on the other hand a continual resistance is present. The actions and effects exercised on the organism cannot always work their way up here [top of drawing]. There is resistance everywhere, and they are pushed back down. What we do in so far as we adhere to physical organs seeks to stream up into the head; but the human organization does not allow it to, stops it. And therefore it also collects and

accumulates in a certain way [red], here forming a kind of astral centre. Again, this develops very markedly at the time of puberty, and so, at the same place where this etheric heart—our own now—formed, we also have an astral configuration in which all our actions converge and concentrate. From puberty onwards, a central organ is created in which all our actions, all our human activity is concentrated. Thus in the same region where our heart lies, all our activity is concentrated—astrally now, not physically or etherically. And the important thing is that at the time when puberty begins—since astral occurrences coincide roughly, though not exactly, with physical ones—this etheric heart has already developed sufficiently for it to absorb the forces that develop here from activity and work in the external world. And so, given this real occurrence within the human being, we can say that from puberty onwards all human activity connects via the astral body with the etheric heart, the organ that developed from images, reflections of the cosmos. All this connects and comes together there.

This is a very important phenomenon indeed, for if you consider all this you find a convergence between what we do in the world and the cosmos. In so far as the etheric world is concerned, you have a concentrated cosmos in the heart; but at the same time also, in relation to the astral world, you have a concentration of what we do, our actions. Here the cosmos and its occurrences unite with human karma. Only in the region of the heart is there such an intimate correspondence of the astral body and the etheric body with the whole human organism. Here the whole world of which we bring an image in our etheric body into this life at birth is contained as essence, and everything we do and absorb permeates this whole world. Through these convergences and correspondences, an opportunity arises during the whole of a human life for human activity continually to connect and engage with this essence of images and reflections of the cosmos.

When we pass through the portal of death, this etheric-astral configuration in which the heart floats, as we can say, contains everything that we take with us in our further life of spirit and soul after we have laid aside the physical body and this etheric weft. And—because this contains the substance of the whole cosmos, which in the heart's ether body was merely contracted—as we now grow spiritually ever larger we can pass our whole karma over to the cosmos. What originated in the cosmos and became etheric configuration, what contracted in the heart and became essence, seeks its way into the cosmos again. We spread ourselves out in the whole cosmos, and are absorbed into the soul world, undergoing what I described in my *Theosophy*[22] as the passage through the soul world and then spirit land. When we study the growth and development of the human organization, we can in fact say that in the region of the heart the cosmos and the earth unite, and do so by virtue of the cosmic quality being integrated into the etheric, readying itself there to assimilate our actions, everything we do. Having passed through the portal of death we go out into the cosmos with what formed through an inner permeation of the etheric with human activity, and return again to a new cosmic existence.

Thus we can describe in very tangible ways how a human being approaches his physical body, lives his way into it, and how he can withdraw again from this physical body because his deeds and actions give him the strength to make cohere what he only developed as essence out of the cosmos.

The physical body is of course formed within the physical earthly world through the forces of inheritance, that is, through the forces of embryonic and foetal development. What we bring down with us from the world of spirit connects and unites with this, after we have first drawn our etheric body towards us. We unite with this on the one hand. But within the astral element, a wondrous configuration we have brought with us, there also dwells the I that has passed through many lives on earth and undergone a whole process of evolution. This I lives in a certain sympathy connection—the phrase refers to something very real—with everything contained in the astral body's configuration. And as these configurations slip into the organs of the physical body as I described, the I retains this sympathy and develops it also towards the organs, increasingly occupying and taking possession of them. But these inherited characteristics I spoke about are present there, and the I's relationship to them is an external one. But gradually the I does slip with its astral body into the physical body's organs, so that the following occurs as it does so. Whereas previously the I in the child was present in what I will call an external way in and through blood circulation, now, increasingly, it strongly connects inwardly with blood circulation until this intensifying connection has come about most fully by the time of puberty. And whereas you have here an astral configuration around the etheric and physical heart, an astral configuration here therefore [drawing, p. 91, orange], the I takes another path: it slips into the lungs. With the blood vessels that pass from the lungs to the heart, the I increasingly approaches the heart. Inwardly connected with blood circulation, the I increasingly follows its path. Via the I forces running together with the blood circulation, the I again engages in what has been formed from the union of the etheric and the astral heart; and here an etheric element from the cosmos grows together with an astral element belonging to us ourselves. I said before that this astral body gradually comes to contain a great deal since all our deeds are inscribed in it. But since the I has a sympathy and affinity with all that the astral body accomplishes, the aims and ideas which instigate our actions are also inscribed. A complete union therefore really does come about between our karma and the laws at work in the cosmos.

Of all these things that occur within us, people today know precious little. The heart is in this respect an unknown country. People know about what happens here in the physical world, and regard this as natural law; and they know about moral actions, regarding this as moral law. And yet everything of a moral nature that occurs within us, and everything of a physical nature on the other hand, unites in the human heart. These two realms that run along separate, parallel tracks in the modern view, morality and natural law, in fact can be found to unite in the human heart if we learn to understand what occurs there, albeit in a far more hidden way than in the palpable phenomenon of second dentition. We inherit teeth, and we subsequently form teeth out of our organism. The milk teeth fall away, while the others stay for the rest of our life. The milk teeth tend to degenerate, and would not last if they did not fall out. Our permanent teeth are largely destroyed by external circumstances, including of course external conditions within the organism itself. Similarly, though invisibly, our etheric heart is given over to decay at puberty, and we gain a kind of permanent heart, a kind of ether heart. Only this permanent etheric heart is fully suited to taking up our activity in the full sense. This is why it is a very different thing if someone dies before puberty or after it. If he dies before puberty then the only tendency present in him is for what he did on earth to be bequeathed as karmic heredity. Certain things can be incorporated into the karma of a child who dies before puberty, but this always has a somewhat undefined and iridescent quality. Proper forming of karma only occurs from the moment when the astral heart fully engages with the etheric heart so that they merge. This also is, if I can put it like this, the organism of karma. At death, you see, what is concentrated in us, what has been bound together, grows ever more cosmic, and later will be incorporated into the human being again out of the cosmos in the next life on earth. This means that everything we do not only affects ourselves, is not just our own concern. Something that comes from the cosmos is incorporated into us, and retains the tendency, after death, to pass our deeds back to the cosmos. Because of this, karmic laws work actively in the forming of our karma, so that when our next life on earth begins we bear with us into this new life the effects of what the cosmos has made of our deeds.

Lecture 7

27 May 1922

TODAY I want to highlight the fact that in diverse times people have been able to gain knowledge of the kind I described yesterday in relation to the development of the human etheric and astral body. An account of how we acquire such perceptions can also, you see, give us some insight into human nature, our relationship with the world, and so forth. It certainly isn't necessary for everyone to be able to undertake such things, but accounts of how people have proceeded, or still proceed, when doing so sheds light in turn on findings that are of great importance for all. There is a very great difference between the way in which people gained supersensible knowledge in very ancient times and how they do today. I have often pointed out that ancient humanity possessed a certain instinctive clairvoyance, which gradually, through various intermediate stages, developed into the view of the world which we must call our own today. Out of this general consciousness, a certain higher consciousness can be developed. In the second part of my *Occult Science*,[23] *Knowledge of the Higher Worlds*,[24] and other books, I described how a person can acquire higher knowledge if he rightly understands the time he lives in, and his relationship to this era. But today I would like to give you an account that relates to what I described yesterday.

Looking back to very ancient times of humanity's evolution, and the spiritual endeavours of those times, one of the things we find is the spiritual path that existed in the ancient Orient, in the culture whose later periods became known as Indian culture. Today many people are returning to this path because they fail to see that every epoch must find its own, different way of penetrating supersensible worlds.

On a previous occasion I also suggested here that of the whole mass of humankind living at that era—which I have called the epoch of ancient India in my *Occult Science*—certain individuals developed inner powers in a way appropriate for those days, and that these powers led them up into supersensible worlds. One of these paths, which I described here in a different context, was called the yoga path.

We can best understand the yoga path if we first consider the rest of humanity at that time, from which emerged the yogi who sought this path of higher knowledge. In those more ancient times of humanity's evolution, ordinary consciousness was quite different from today. Today we look out into the world, for instance perceiving colours with our eyes, hearing tones and so forth. We seek the laws of this sense world but are aware that if we go further, seeking to live our way into outer phenomena with, we can say, our spirit and soul, we are then drawing on our imagination. In ancient times this was not so. At that time, as we know, people saw more in the outer world than people today ordinarily see. In thunder and lightning, in every planet and star, in every realm of nature, ancient people at the same time discerned spirit and soul. They perceived spiritual beings, albeit of a lower kind, in all the realms of earth, air, water and so on. Intellectuals and academics today think that these ancient people dreamed whatever they perceived of this kind, that their imagination imbued their environment with these entities. This is called 'animism'.

Well, it betrays a poor knowledge of human nature, and above all the human nature of those times, to think that people simply dreamed up all kinds of beings in their imagination when they saw them in lightning and thunder, springs and rivers, wind and weather. No, that is not the case. They saw them. Just as we see red and blue, or hear C sharp and G, so these people of ancient times perceived realities of spirit and soul in external phenomena. This was as natural for them as it is for us today to see red and blue. But something else was also connected with it: the fact that in those times they had no clear sense of self.

The clear sense of self we normally possess today, which fills us through and through, was lacking in those far-off times. People did not distinguish themselves from the external world. Though they did not express it like this, these ancient people perceived roughly what my hand would see if it had consciousness—that it is not separate and autonomous, that it is only a part of my organism. They felt themselves to be part of the whole universe, and made little distinction between their own human nature and the rest of their surroundings. Let us imagine a person of those times walking along a river. Today if we do this, walking in the direction of the current's flow, as modern, intelligent people we have the feeling of our legs carrying us along without any sense that this is connected with the river itself. In ancient times a person did not usually feel this. As he walked downriver—which was a natural thing for him to do—he sensed the spiritual entities connected with the river's downward flow in a way that resembles how a swimmer today will feel borne up by the water, that is, by something material in nature. He felt himself led downwards by something spiritual. This is just a random example. Everything people experienced in their surroundings was conceived and sensed in a similar way—they felt sustained, or we can say impelled, by the gods of wind, water and everything else in the external world. They felt the natural elements within them. Such a close affinity with nature is something we have lost. Instead we have gradually acquired a strong sense of a separate self.

The yogi scholar emerged from the whole mass of those who experienced the world in this way. He undertook certain exercises. Whereas these were fitting for the human nature of ancient times, they later fell into great decadence and were then used almost entirely for harmful purposes. These are exercises I have often referred to, those of yogic breathing. But what I will now describe was a right and proper path into higher worlds only for people in very ancient oriental culture.

In ordinary life, our breathing is unconscious. We breathe in, hold our breath and breathe out. Only if we suffer from some kind of disorder do we become aware of our breathing. Ordinarily it remains a largely unconscious process. Now, through certain periods of practice, the yogi transformed breathing into a conscious inner process by altering its whole rhythm and the length of time taken for breathing in, holding the breath and breathing out again. He made the inbreath longer, held the breath for longer, and breathed out again in a different tempo. In other words, he gave himself a different breathing rhythm from the usual one. This made his whole breathing more conscious. We can say that he lived into his breathing. And the feeling of himself that he gained was that of continually following and accompanying the inbreath, the spreading out of the breath in his body, and the outbreath again. By this means he entered into his breathing with his whole being of soul.

If we wish to understand what this achieved, we can put it like this: when we breathe in, the breath enters our organism, then passes through the spinal column into the brain, there spreading out in processes that occur in the nerve and sense organism. Thus when we think as human beings, the tools of this thinking are never just the nerve-sense organism, but the latter is continually also infused with rhythm; pulse—the breathing process, the breathing rhythm—streams and surges through it. We do not think without this breathing rhythm rhythmically pervading our nerve-sense process. This of course remains unconscious since the whole breathing process is normally unconscious in people today.

In the yogi this altered breathing was consciously drawn into the nerve-sense process, giving him an experience of an inner occurrence composed of what arose through this nerve-sense process and what surged and swirled through the brain and also the senses. By this means he also brought the soul faculty of his thinking into the breathing rhythm.

Something very particular approached the yogi in consequence.

We can say that he radiated thinking, otherwise scarcely felt to be [other than?] a head process, into his whole organism. He not only thought but he felt how his thought, like some kind of little creature, ran through the breathing process he had artificially elicited.

Thus he experienced thinking not only as something unfolding in a logical and shadowy way, but in its accompaniment of the breathing process. When he breathed in he felt that he was drawing something in from the outer world which he allowed to flow into his thinking process. We can say that he encompassed with his thoughts the air he sucked in with the inbreath, and then diffused throughout his organism. This gave rise in the yogi to an enhanced I experience, an enhanced sense of self. In a feeling way he diffused his thinking through his whole inner being. By this means he became aware of his thinking in the air, in the regular motions of breathing that occurred within him.

This had a very particular outcome for him. Today, feeling ourselves to be within the sense world, it is quite right that we have in our thinking something that we scarcely observe. Our senses convey to us what exists in the outer world, and when we look back at ourselves we perceive at least parts of ourself. By this means we acquire a picture of the way in which we exist in the external world between birth and death. But the yogi, we can say, radiated his soul-thinking through his breathing process. He sent this whole soul thinking more inwards, which allowed a distinct sense of self, a particular I-experience to emerge from his soul. However, he did not experience this as a human being in a natural environment between birth and death but, by virtue of radiating his soul thinking into the breathing process, he felt himself as if recalled to the time before he had descended to the earth—to the time when he was a being of spirit and soul in a world of spirit and soul. Just as a person today, in his ordinary awareness can, if he has a particularly vivid memory of something that happened ten years ago, feel himself back into this occurrence and its whole context—let's say re-experiencing the woods where this experience happened—and can invoke the whole mood of that event, so the yogi, by changing his breathing process, touched back into the whole environment where he had been a being of spirit and soul within a world of spirit and soul. He felt quite differently about the world in this experience from how he felt as a person here on earth. What overcame him at these moments, arising from the affinity between this awoken self and the whole universe, gave rise to those wonderful ancient poems which include, for example, the beautiful *Bhagvad Gita*.

If you read these wonderful accounts in the *Bhagvad Gita* about the human self and the way in which this self accompanies everything, how it immerses itself in all natural phenomena, in all the varied secrets of the world, how it is contained in all things, this conveys the memories, invoked through the yoga breathing process, of the soul when it was still only soul alone and lived in a spiritual universe. You will only read this *Bhagvad Gita* rightly if you keep in mind as you do so that the soul transposed back into the world of spirit, with its enhanced sense of self, is uttering all this: all that was exhaled in the breath of Krishna or other ancient initiates who achieved such a sense of self.

And so we can say that these wise ancients raised themselves from the populace of the time and strictly detached their self from the external world. They sundered it. But they did not do this through, say, egoistic thoughts, but by a transformed breathing process that accompanied the soul's immersion in the inner rhythm of the air in the body. This was the way in which people of ancient times sought to enter the world of spirit.

In later eras this path changed. In ancient times people engaged in the breathing practice I have described, feeling how the thoughts they immersed in the streams of breath passed like snakes through the currents of breathing. This enabled them to experience their self in the world's universal weft. The revelation they experienced was given utterance in certain words and phrases. They noticed that they spoke differently when they used language to reveal what they experienced in this way. But gradually what I have described here—an experience anchored in the breathing process itself—dwindled, was no longer so strongly felt. Gradually instead it came to seem that the words exhaled and uttered themselves, that the words arranged themselves into chanted verses, quite naturally becoming speech-song, chanted recitation.

The altered breathing process, therefore, gave rise to words sustained and carried by it, which people then in a sense detached from it to form mantric verses, mantras. Whereas the key thing in more ancient times was the breathing process itself and the experience of it, the emphasis shifted to these mantras. This entered tradition, passed into people's historical awareness, and this largely gave rise later to the rhythms, pulse and so forth of poetry.

But the experience of early Greek times—of an intuitive sense of the lawfulness of language, giving rise to the hexameter,[25] to the pentameter,[26]—can be traced back to an earlier era, and then we discover an ancient experience of breathing. And this was destined to carry the human being away from the world in which he lives between birth and death, and back into a world of spirit and soul.

It cannot be our mission today to seek our way into the world of spirit in the way practised in ancient times. Not via the breath, but on a more inward path, more that of thought itself, we should live our way upward into worlds of spirit. Today the right approach, therefore, is through meditation and concentration to transform the merely logical context of our thoughts and images into, let us say, a musical context, doing so within thinking itself. Modern meditation is always initially a thought experience, a transition from one thought to another, from one idea to another.

Whereas the ancient Indian yogi passed from one form of breathing to another, today we must try to immerse our whole soul vividly, for instance, in the colour red. This remains in the realm of thought. Then we live our way into blue, alternating rhythmically from red to blue, from blue to red, from red to blue. This is a thought rhythm—not as it unfolds in logical thinking but a much more living thinking.

We must practise such exercises for a sufficient period (the old yogi also had to practise his exercises for a long time) and experience the alternating rhythm, a swinging between the two inner qualities of red and blue. In other words, you can follow the guidance such as that offered in my book *Knowledge of the Higher Worlds.* Rather than driving the breath into the neurosensory process, you stay within thinking itself, with the neurosensory process itself, and bring this into inner momentum and rhythm, and into an inner alteration of quality. If you do so you achieve the very opposite of what the ancient yogi did. In a sense he merged the thinking process with the breathing process, making them one. Today, instead, we try to dissolve the last connection between the breathing process and the thinking process, which is anyway very unconscious. If you form thoughts about your natural surroundings in your everyday awareness, you never merely have a neurosensory process in your thoughts but the breath is always also involved. You can think by virtue of the fact that your breath continually surges and streams through your neurosensory process.

All modern meditation practice is focused entirely on releasing thinking from the breathing process. But in doing so, as well as detaching it from our inner rhythm we then also gradually connect it with an outer rhythm. In releasing thinking from the rhythm of breathing as our meditation today aims to do, we allow thinking, we can say, to stream into the rhythm of the outer world. The yogi returned to his own rhythms. Nowadays we return to the rhythm of the outer world. Read the first exercises in *Knowledge of the Higher Worlds*, where I show how, for instance, one should attentively observe the germination and growth of a plant. This meditation aims to release thinking from the breathing, and to let it immerse itself in the plant's own forces of growth.

Thinking should go out into the rhythm that pervades the outer world. But the moment thinking really frees itself in this way from bodily functions, where it sunders itself from the breath, where it gradually unites with outer rhythm, it immerses itself not in sensory perceptions, the sensory qualities of things, but in the spiritual nature of diverse things.

Let us imagine a plant—green, with red flowers. That is what your eye tells you, and then your powers of reason reflect on it. That is how our everyday consciousness lives. We develop a different kind of awareness when we sunder our thinking from the breath, and connect it instead with what is outside us. This thinking learns to resonate with the plant as it grows, as its flower opens, and as—in a rose for instance—it passes from green into red. It resonates out into the spiritual reality that underlies all the diverse things of the external world.

You see, that is the difference between modern meditation practice and the yoga exercises of a very ancient time. There are many transitional stages between these two, of course, but I will speak now only of these two opposite extremes. As a person gradually lives out into this outer rhythm, the following occurs.

The yogi immersed himself in his own breathing process. He sank into himself and by this means he acquired the self as a memory. We can say that he remembered what he had once been before he descended to the earth. We, on the other hand, convey our soul out of the body and connect with what lives outside us in rhythm, and thus spiritually. Thereby we can now observe, perceive, what we were before we descended to the earth.

That's the difference. I'll draw it schematically: the yogi here [drawing 1, p. 111, white] developed a strong sense of I [red]. With this sense of self he recalled what he was before he descended to the earth, when he lived in a soul-spiritual environment [blue]. His current of memory returned there.

Here now we have the modern supersensible investigator [drawing 2, p. 111, white]. In his case he goes out of his body [blue] and thus lives in the rhythm of the outer world; and he can now perceive as an outward entity what he was prior to descending to the earth.

Thus knowledge of the pre-birth state was somewhat like memory recall in ancient times, whereas today, if we undertake this in the right way, we perceive and observe our nature in the pre-birth state [red]. That's the difference. That was one way in which the yogi raised himself into worlds of spirit. Another was to put his body into certain positions. For instance he might practise holding his arms

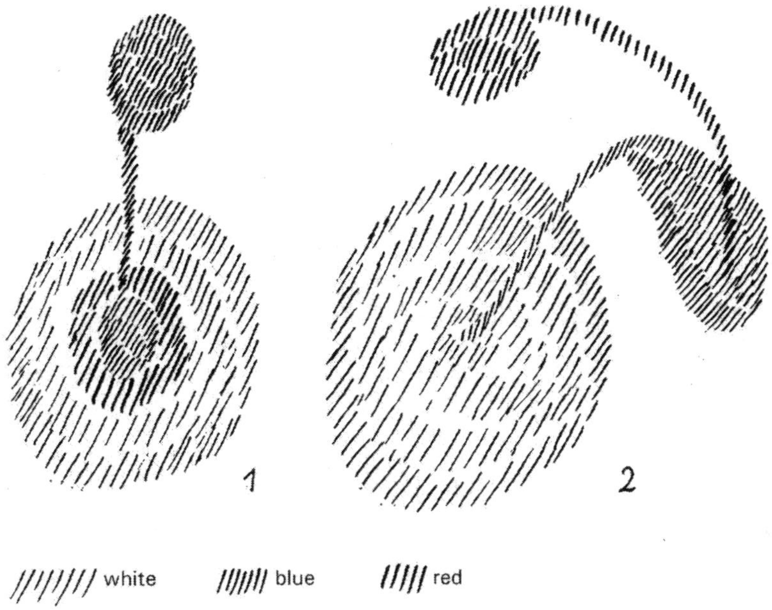

outstretched for a long time, or crossing one leg over the other and as it were sitting on his own legs. What did this achieve?

This enabled him to perceive what is conveyed by senses that we scarcely consider today. As we know, the human being does not only have five but twelve senses.[27] Apart from the ordinary senses, we also have a sense of balance, for instance. I have often spoken about this. By means of this sense we perceive how to maintain balance so that we do not fall to left or right, backwards or forwards. Just as one perceives colours, so we must also perceive our balance, otherwise we would constantly slip or fall to one side or the other. Someone who is drunk or feeling faint does not perceive this, and therefore tumbles about. Now to bring this sense of balance to his awareness, the yogi assumed certain postures, thereby developing a fine, subtle sense of the various directions of space. We speak of up and down, right and left, back and front, as if they were all much of a muchness. The yogi gradually developed a very strong, fine awareness of distinctive qualities in these orientations, through the postures he assumed for longer periods.

In particular he developed a fine sense for these other senses I spoke of apart from the five senses. When these senses are experienced, they have a far more spiritual character than the ordinary senses. And by this means the yogi found his way in turn into a perception of the directions of space.

We need to acquire this again, though in a different way. For reasons I will elaborate on another time, we cannot undertake a practice such as that of ancient yoga. But by engaging in thinking exercises as I just described them, which can release themselves from our breathing and enter into outward rhythm, we can experience the different qualities of each direction. We can experience what it means for the animal to have a horizontal spine while we have a vertical one. In regard to ordinary inorganic nature, we know that the magnetic needle only points in a north-south direction, and that this orientation has a particular significance for magnetism: the magnetic needle, neutral in all other respects, finds this position and shows it to be a distinctive orientation. By leading our thoughts out into external rhythm, we learn to perceive how different it is if the spine lies horizontally or vertically. We learn all this in thoughts themselves, remaining within the thought realm. The Indian yogi also learned this by crossing his legs, sitting up upon his own legs and holding his arms up at the same time. In other words, bodily positions taught him the invisible significance of spatial directions. Space is not a random assembly but is organized in all directions such that these directions have varying qualities. Exercises such as those I just

described, that lead people into the higher world, are ones that tend more towards the thought aspect.

But there are also exercises that tend in the other direction, and here, amongst the manifold exercises that exist in this field, we find those of ascetic privation, where the functions of the physical body are dampened and all kinds of suffering or deprivation are imposed on the body. By this means we can say that the physical body was taken away from its normal functions. People today, who endeavour to enter their physical organism as thoroughly as possible, have no idea what ascetics of more ancient times achieved in this way. Whenever the ancient ascetic painfully suppressed this or that bodily function, his spirit and soul withdrew from his organism.

You see, if you live in the normal way, your soul and spirit are bound up with your physical organism in a way that is fit and proper for the human being between birth and death. If you ascetically suppress bodily functions, something similar happens to you as happens, to a lesser degree, when someone injures themselves in some way.

Now if you know what happens with modern people if they feel a little pain, it will be clear there is a world of difference between this and what ancient ascetics endured to release their soul organism. Their soul organism, driven out of the body by their ascetic practice, began to have experiences in the world of spirit. It is largely by this means that all of the great religious ideas of olden times were obtained.

Modern exponents of religious consciousness simplify things—they declare these religious ideas to be a fiction, and this is because they hold to the principle that such insights should not cause pain to the enquirer. This was not the point of view of ancient seekers, who were clear that if a person stands fully within his physical organism—which of course is right and proper for his earthly work, and by no means do I suggest that it would be right to become estranged from the world—he cannot have any experience of the world of spirit. The ancient ascetics sought this experience by dulling and deadening the body, and even inflicting pain on it. Whenever they drove out the soul and spirit from a bodily limb through pain, this portion experienced spirit and soul in the world of spirit. The great religions were not founded painlessly but through deep suffering.

Today, insights that have arisen in the course of human evolution are assimilated through faith. Today people make a nice, clean distinction between knowledge on the one hand, scientific knowledge of the external world which is acquired through the head—the head has a thick skull, which feels no pain especially since scientific findings pass through extremely fine-meshed concepts—and, on the other hand, honourable traditions that people 'take on faith', as they say. But from a certain point of view we ought also to say that the difference between knowledge and faith amounts to this: that today people wish only to grant validity to what does not cause pain as they acquire it; and through faith, which does not cause pain either, they seek to acquire something that was also once knowledge but of a kind that does not belong to the sense world. Yet this knowledge was originally discovered by means of great pain and suffering.

Well, the ascetic path is not suitable for modern people either, despite everything I have said. We will consider why this is on another occasion. But it is certainly possible to intervene in the will growth forces in one's own individuality by disciplining the will, by taking in hand the development that otherwise only occurs through life and education. For instance, if we say to ourselves that in five years' time we must have acquired a new habit of life and, if during these five years, we direct all the power of our will to do so, focusing our will on perfecting ourselves inwardly, then we release the spirit and soul from the body without resorting to asceticism. Initially we feel that what we must undertake in this process of self-perfecting can only be accomplished through our own continuous activity.

Every day we must accomplish something inwardly—perhaps seemingly small things, but they must still be done with unwavering effort and irresistible patience. Often when you suggest to people that, say, they cultivate a very particular thought each morning, they are at first full of eagerness to do so. But before long these efforts lapse and they rely on things going by themselves instead. You can see that this practice becomes mechanical, because they do not wish to apply the stronger effort that will become ever more necessary. Firstly therefore, we have to overcome this resistance of our own sluggishness, and then comes the resistance that originates in an objective reality. It is as if one were trying to work one's way through something very dense, and then a real inner experience dawns—of a thinking that has gradually been developing, that has come to life, that can now perceive the diverse qualities of spatial directions and in fact everything of a living nature, a thinking that finds its way out into the rhythm of the external world. And in consequence we find that things hurt us, that every insight we achieve is painful.

People today who seek the path into higher worlds can easily have the following experience. They begin their practice. The first, tentative insights come. This hurts; and so they think they are sick. Naturally that is what we think if something is hurting, that we are ill. But in achieving higher knowledge, we can sometimes feel much pain, and yet we are not sick. However, rather than advancing on the path required by higher knowledge—for our soul pain grows ever greater—it is easier and more comfortable to find a cure for it, to soothe the pain rather than continuing in one's striving. We go and get a prescription instead of pursuing our path further. This is much more comfortable of course, but it will not help us further on the path of knowledge. This immersion in pain, in suffering, becomes an inner path of the soul for modern people, unfolding purely in the soul realm. The body does not initially really participate in it, in so far as it remains robust, strong and able to cope with the outer world, as is normally the case today. But when a person begins to allow his insights to draw towards him as something that brings with it suffering, he enters the regions of spiritual life in which the great religious truths once originated. The great religious truths, that is, those that give us a religious sensibility through the impression made by the higher world, the supersensible world, the world in which for instance our immortality is rooted, are ones that cannot be achieved without painful inner experiences.

Having been achieved in this way, they can in turn be passed on to ordinary human minds. People today are resistant to such truths for the simple reason that they sense such things are not ones they wish to countenance.

Some people, for instance, might react very badly to what I said yesterday: that everything a person does, even what he commissions others to do, is inscribed in this transforming astral body, which then engages with, intervenes in the etheric heart. The very thought of it can make one inwardly tremulous. And the great truths ask us, in a sense, for a courage of soul that is stalwart enough to say: If you experience these things, then you must be willing to achieve insight through privation and pain.

I do not say this to discourage you, though it will discourage many today. It is simply the truth. What use would it be to tell people they can retain their comfortable well-being as they enter the highest worlds if, in fact, doing so requires one to overcome oneself, to meet and overcome suffering?

Today, my dear friends, I have tried to describe to you how we advance further into our deeper humanity. This human soul and spirit is deeply concealed within us and we must first work our way through to it. But even if people do not undertake this themselves, they must know that this core being does lie concealed in them; and the needs of our time must show them the true nature and course of the things we described yesterday.

Such things can only be discovered on paths of knowledge that I have again hinted at today, which have unfolded in different ways in ancient and modern times.

Tomorrow we will build further on the observations from today and yesterday, combining them in a way that will hopefully lead us further into worlds of spirit.

LECTURE 8

28 MAY 1922

TODAY, hearkening back first to our observations yesterday and the day before, I would like to consider some aspects of the future of human evolution in so far as this is dependent on a certain relationship we will develop with certain spiritual powers as the earth's future develops. The day before yesterday we saw how the inner human being appears to closer, more detailed observation, how in this closer study we can gain insight into how, in our physical, soul and spiritual human nature, two things are bound together: firstly what, in a sense, belongs to the outer world, in so far as this world is understood as one of etheric powers and beings which we draw towards us for our own etheric body as we descend to the earthly world. This nature of ours, belonging more to the outer world but rooting itself within us, combines with what we ourselves accomplish on earth—in other words, our deeds and our karma.

Then yesterday we saw how at various stages and eras of human evolution people have been able to develop, and should develop, various kinds of relationship, insight and affinity with the world of spirit.

Now I have often mentioned that our modern era is one where a new stream of spiritual life simply seeks entry into human existence on earth. Our current stage of human evolution needs to form a transition between the primarily intellectual age that started in the first third of the fifteenth century, which has now largely ended, and a future dedicated to the spirit. In this intellectual era, the prime focus was on humanity developing its powers of reason as a self-sufficient capacity, based on the outward observation of nature and technology.

Great and magnificent things were achieved in this respect in recent centuries. But everything of this nature was oriented to human reason, to the intellectual element in human evolution. And the legacy of this intellectual element still lives among us today, though I have to say that it is no longer creative.

This intellectual life was creative to the highest degree at the time of Copernicus, Galileo, Giordano Bruno through into the nineteenth century. The creative intellect gave rise to great human deeds in recent centuries, especially in western civilization.

If we study things without prejudice we can discern even outwardly that the creative power of intelligence has waned significantly in recent centuries. Humanity no longer, as it were, unites this intellect, this reasoning faculty with enthusiasm. The soul-imbued reason that was practised for centuries lives on through a certain cultural inertia. People still think on the old tracks. But the intellect produces nothing new. We can notice this particularly in young people today. As I say, unprejudiced observation can show this. If you look back to the younger academic generation of the 80s in the last century [1880s]—and this relates no doubt to the whole of western civilization (certainly it was not true of all, but was apparent in those who mattered)—you would have seen that a young person who had learned a thing or two and began to speak elicited a certain pleasure in his listeners. One was eager to see what he would say as he went on speaking. This is no longer so. The change has come about very discernibly in recent decades. When a young person today comes fresh from academe and starts speaking, one simply has no desire to listen for long, since one knows in advance what he will say—it all runs automatically. People's brains no longer appear to be in lively spate, in the full flow of intellect. One has a sense that the activity of intelligence has slid downwards from the head into deeper regions. Anyone who observes the world with an open mind today can discover this through mere outward observation. The human intellect has acquired a certain mechanical quality, and this intelligence now springs forth from regions of the human organization other than just the head. Well, this is because, as I said, this intelligence was originally elemental and because the fact that humanity should develop intelligence through this era, from the fifteenth to the nineteenth century, is implicit in the whole lawfulness of the world.

But now a spiritual stream is seeking entry into the earthly life of human beings from higher regions of world existence. The faculty of reason, now needing no further development, is to be fertilized by this spiritual stream. And it inevitably depends on human beings themselves whether they open their hearts, their souls to what, if you like, must enter from the world of spirit into the earthly world through many portals. But this means that human beings must again acquire a receptivity for perceiving spirit in the whole of nature.

Remember, as we mentioned yesterday, that if we look back to ancient civilizations, we find that all humanity perceived spirit and soul in external phenomena—in every star, cloud, thunder and lightning, in all natural creatures.

Ancient yoga practice emerged from this, raised itself from it. As I described yesterday, the yogi tried to penetrate to the self. By the practice of inner exercises he tried to develop a certain sense of self, an I-consciousness—which is natural to us today, for it is innate in us and our education cultivates it. The yogi first had to develop this sense in himself.

Now my dear friends, do not imagine that you may count yourself equal to a yogi with your ordinary modern I-consciousness! There is a difference between working one's way through to something through one's own human efforts or possessing it as innate endowment. If, as the yogi did, people first had to work their way up to self-awareness then, through this inner practice, they participated in great, mighty cosmic processes, patterns and laws. This is not the case if we are simply placed into the sphere of self-awareness. To stand naturally at a stage of human evolution is by no means the same as achieving this stage through inner practice.

And you can see from yesterday's presentation that humanity must gradually come to insights that proceed, for example, from releasing the whole system of thinking from the breathing process, since then the system of thinking, as I described yesterday, lives its way into the outer rhythm of the cosmos. By releasing itself from subjectivity, the system of thinking immerses itself in the rhythms of the cosmos. And so the yogi crept deeper into himself by—if we can put it like this—coupling his thinking system with the breathing system, identifying with what the spirit and soul in him could unfold on the waves of breathing's inner rhythm. We on the other hand must pour our thinking out into the world, give ourselves up to the world so as to participate in all the rhythms that pulsate through the mineral, plant, animal and human worlds right up to the world of the hierarchies. We have to live our way into the outward rhythm of existence. But by doing so, we will also come to insights that in turn teach humanity something about what underlies external science.

Today we practise physics, chemistry and biology; and in thousands upon thousands of popular accounts, which reach the furthest-flung village, people receive information about how the world appears to a combination of sense observation and intellect. But an age must begin when humanity once again learns what underlies all that can be discovered through external observation and the intellect.

It does not matter whether we speak, along with the ancients, of the four elements, earth, water, air and fire, or speak in purely physical terms with modern minds about solid bodies, fluid bodies, gaseous bodies and temperature. The names we give to these things do not matter for the purposes we are pursuing today. You see, when we speak today of the external world, of solids, fluids, gases, we are speaking in terms of the outward composition, decomposition, separation, etc. of substances. But we must remember that an elemental spiritual reality underlies all solid matter. Modern enlightened minds may ridicule the gnomes that ancient humanity discerned in all earthly substance; but when, through living our way out into the rhythm of the world, rather than formulating merely logical, abstract contexts of thought, we gain different insights again, we will rediscover the elemental beings contained in all solid, earthly substance. The primary characteristic of the elemental beings in the earth's solid matter is that of cleverness, cunning, slyness, the one-sided development of the intellect. We can say this: that in the solid element of earth live spiritual-elemental beings who are cleverer than humankind, far cleverer. The most intellectually acute people are not as clever as the supersensible beings who inhabit the realm of solid earthly substance. We can say that these beings are actually composed of cleverness alone. We consist of flesh and blood, while these beings are made of superior cleverness. They have the strange characteristic of multiplicity. If one is able to examine a suitable earth element to study the activities of these elemental beings of cleverness, one can, as it were, squeeze them out like water from a sponge, in a soul-spiritual sense; and they pour out, these beings. There is no end to them—a great wealth of them is present.

Even trying to count these beings who live in the solid constituents of earth is somewhat difficult. In trying to enumerate them in the ordinary way it becomes apparent that they won't let themselves be counted, one, two, three, four, five like eggs or cherries. By the time you have reached three, say, they are no longer three but far more. You won't get very far with counting them by means familiar on the ordinary physical plane. And if we tried to apply the usual four processes in counting them, these beings would play the strangest tricks on us. If you placed two of them on one side, and two on another and said 'two times two is four', you would find this wasn't true; as you were making your calculations these beings would, through their superordinate cleverness, present themselves instead as seven or eight, forcing us to conclude that two times two is eight or something along those lines.

The idiosyncrasies of these entities therefore even thwart counting. We have to recognize that the intellect humanity has developed in modern times may be very fine, but these beings, with their super-intelligence, display a degree of superiority to this intellect. They even display a superiority to straightforward enumeration.

When we come to the fluid element, to water, these elemental entities primarily elaborate what we have developed in our feeling and sensibility. Our human feelings are actually a long way behind those of the beings who inhabit the element of water, of fluid. We may take pleasure in a red rose. A certain feeling fills us when foliage rustles on a tree. But these beings accompany all the fluid in plant sap rising in the rose up to its flower; they have a full experience of this red. They accompany the world's processes in a far more intimate way than we do. Our feelings remain outside things, whereas theirs are within phenomena, and inwardly accompany them.

The elemental air beings have developed to a higher capacity what we possess in our will. It is a fine thing of course when a chemist discovers the atomic weight of hydrogen, oxygen, nitrogen, how hydrogen and oxygen combine, how they can be analysed in turn—how for example one analyses water or chloride of lime. All that is very fine, but underlying all this live spiritual, elemental beings. And humankind will have to acquire an understanding of the idiosyncrasies of this elemental world. In the age when human beings developed their intellect, these elemental beings were to some degree marginalized. Since the first third of the fifteenth century, as I have said, and up to the end of the nineteenth century, humanity developed the intellect; and in so far as the intellect came to play a creative part in human culture, these beings who live in the elements could not do a great deal. Because the elemental beings of solid substance were compelled to hold themselves back, in a sense, and leave the intellect to the devices of humankind, these beings also kept the others back as well, those of water and air. But now humanity is entering a time when the intellect becomes decadent. This is the case; we are living at a time when the intellect in the civilized world is starting to decline. And if humanity does not open itself to the spiritual current's influx from the realm of spirit, human stupor towards this influx will give rise to something that is, indeed, already clearly discernible: these elemental beings will conclude a kind of union and confederacy which hearkens to the leadership of the primarily intellectualizing power of Ahriman.

And if this happens, if these elemental beings place themselves under Ahriman's dominion with the clear aim of opposing human evolution, humanity could not progress further. In this case it would be possible for ahrimanic powers in union with the beings of the earth's elements to undertake something quite different from what they were originally destined to do. The earth would not become what I described in my book *Occult Science* as the continuing sequence of planetary embodiments of Saturn, Sun, Moon and Earth. You see, the earth will only develop in accordance with original intentions if the human being undertakes his mission in the right way in every age.

Today already we can see how things are going. Those who are somewhat older know that in the past people always conversed with one another in a way that allowed what was within them to be conveyed through ordinary language. People counted on their reason, their intellect being available to them in their 'upper storey', and then on being able to communicate this to others.

Today there are already people who no longer assume that reason is always sitting there in the upper storey. Instead they assume that it has sunk deeper; and then they analyse what someone says instead of taking them at their word. While misguided, psychoanalysing people like this is a kind of admission that reason has slid somewhat deeper in us, into deeper regions of human nature. And in this age of the intellect's decline, people—or at least this is beginning to show itself in some—no longer like it if one addresses their intellect. They like being analysed because they do not wish their head to participate in what their soul is really expressing.

It leads nowhere to consider these things from an external and superficial point of view—not much will emerge if we do so. We have to view things as we just have done, by placing them into the whole context of the cosmos. Only then do things become clear. Psychoanalysis may have some good aspects from the point of view I described yesterday: people no longer just take for granted things that they used to, and go to see an analyst. But the cures needed by people today are too numerous to be devised. External, material cures do not suffice and so people invent psychological ones, do they not? But all this has to be viewed in a larger context.

From an external point of view, there is no need to object to all the compelling and persuasive insights that psychoanalysis offers. These are not hard to understand—not even from a broader view of the cosmos that leads us to recognize the spiritual current seeking entry into modern civilization, which seeks to replace the declining powers of the rational mind, the decline of the intellect.

Our real task today is to recognize this, though modern human beings are evading it. Only here does it become clear what is involved in such things, which can easily appear outwardly justified in this age of the declining intellect. It will become ever easier to demonstrate all sorts of things, precisely because of this decline and degeneration. The deteriorating intellect will gradually come to demonstrate the justification for all kinds of things. And yet people will increasingly only be able to recognize what is truly justified through insights that come to humanity through spirituality.

That is one aspect which highlights a threat approaching us in humanity's future on earth. On the other hand we must also point out that just as the lower elements of earth, water and air are inhabited by elemental beings, so too are the higher, etheric elements—light, chemical ether, life ether. These higher elemental beings are very different in nature from those of the lower elements. The beings of light, but especially those of life, do not strive for multiplicity. Those who do this most strongly are the elemental beings of earth. The beings of the etheric elements strive for unity. In fact it is hard to distinguish them from each other; there is less emphasis on individuality. These beings all strive to merge with each other, to unite and combine.

An older power of initiation achieved by certain ancient initiates, which gave rise in turn to the deeper teachings of the Old Testament, directed its insights primarily to these etheric elements. This striving of the etheric elements towards unity with each other created the impression that then came to expression in monotheism, in the strict monotheism of Judaism.

This Yahweh religion originally arose primarily through the spiritual vision of ether regions. But in those regions dwell spiritual beings who do not strive apart from each other to become many individuals but who seek instead to form a unity.

Now when these beings too are disregarded by human beings because the latter do not turn towards spirituality, do not acknowledge that as well as the sun in the sky there are etheric beings who reach the earth in sunlight and the sun's warmth, when people do not reach beyond an external grasp of materiality, then these beings find an opportunity to unite with the luciferic. And thus if humanity does not on the one hand deal with the risk of ahrimanic powers uniting with the beings living in the lower elements and, on the other, that of the luciferic powers uniting with the etheric elements' quest for unity, it would be possible for the earth to become quite different in future from what it should have been in accordance with originating intentions.

My dear friends, we cannot say too often that encompassing the spiritual is the destiny of earthly humanity, that something other than what should happen with the earth would do so if human beings do not find their way to the spirit. Around us of course is a material world. But however much we study this material world with our well-developed chemistry and physics, we are only studying what is destined to pass away with earthly existence. What after all is the value of this whole chemistry, this whole field of physics beyond the end of earthly existence? By the end of earthly existence, all pulverized mineral substances will dissolve and pass away, and only plant life, animal life and human life are destined to pass on into Jupiter existence. And so everything accomplished by our magnificent, mighty, modern sciences relates only to transitory things. Humanity needs a knowledge that does not relate to this earthly transience but is connected instead with what passes beyond it.

However much we study things such as the atomic weights of different elements, however much we establish formulae or physical laws, they are all concerned only with things that have transient importance for earthly existence. We must grow beyond this earthly existence through insight into such things as I have described. This is an extraordinarily important and vital undertaking.

If we accord full seriousness to things such as we discovered in our observations yesterday and the day before,[28] and their consequences, then we will want to look in turn again at our anthroposophic movement which endeavours to pay due heed to the spiritual life seeking to flow down upon the earth. We will wish to speak again about the anthroposophic movement itself; and therefore I beg you to let me say a few words about this now.

You can get a sense sometimes that what is happening at present in the anthroposophic movement is quite different from what formerly occurred here. The whole anthroposophic movement emerged really from an esoteric immersion in the spiritual world. When anthroposophy began 20 years ago, at that time still within the Theosophical Society, everything grew out of esoteric foundations really—all the work done in small groups, the lectures, as well as what found its way from these smaller groups into the public domain. We can get a sense of the nature of these esoteric foundations if we look, say, at my 1909 cycle 'The Orient in the Light of the Occident' published in *Die Drei* magazine.[29] This cycle certainly testifies to a strong esoteric impulse.

My dear friends, there are some older members who look back to former times in the anthroposophic movement and feel a degree of dissatisfaction, believing that this esoteric stream has subsided. Actually this isn't true, for it would scarcely be possible nowadays to present anything more esoteric than what has been offered over these three days. We cannot say therefore that there is no longer an engagement with esoteric matters in our inner circles, especially here in Dornach; and this esoteric quality also flows through our public lectures. But this retrospective gaze of older members is not really because the esoteric is no longer present here, no longer flows into these offerings, but because, rather, another phenomenon is apparent.

School of Spiritual Science courses and conferences are now being held in Dornach and in various cities and other places. We held a congress in Stuttgart, and soon there will be one in Vienna. And now, our older members notice that a different tone predominates at these conferences, that anthroposophy is handled differently [from what they are used to], with a certain scientific or academic character. Some of our older members dislike this, and say it doesn't interest them at all. They object that things are presented in too logical and linear a fashion, one thing developed carefully out of another according to the model of modern science. They say they had become accustomed to making great leaps and approaching the world of spirit through a kind of inner understanding, and that they know how to do this. And now people come along and base what they say on the foundations of modern chemistry and physics, and more recently even on mathematical formulae; they proceed logically and sequentially as is the way in modern science, the only difference being that they speak anthroposophically, showing how anthroposophy has no need whatever to avoid scientific discourse. And the older members say that this is of no interest to them.

Yes, my dear friends, this lack of interest is a curious thing. In fact we did not really seek this second stream of anthroposophic life, but it approached us. Anthroposophy today has such a widespread literature that in fact there are many more people in the world who are aware of anthroposophy than one realizes. They just don't like to come forward. But we can tell something from the fact that a book such as my *Occult Science*, which is not—and shouldn't be!—an easy read, has not been written in a way that steals easily and gently into the soul, and is not exactly holiday reading, has gone through 15 editions so far since 1909, and all are now out of print [1922]. Thus anthroposophy emerged into the world, and it was inevitable that scientifically trained or pseudo-scientifically trained people would get to know about it. And one fine day we had to recognize that others were drawing anthroposophy into modern academe and scientific discourse. This was not a matter of choice. It was a *fait accompli* all of a sudden. However inadequately, anthroposophy was being scientifically scrutinized, subjected to critique and disparagement, and held to account academically. It was therefore quite natural that a number of younger friends responded to this by pursuing a course different from older scholars who belonged to our movement.

I may have told you before about an older scholar who drove me nearly to distraction many years ago in a discussion about anthroposophy. The person in question is an extremely scholarly botanist. Well, I was naive enough, or thought that I should seem so for certain reasons, to imagine that it would be best to discuss anthroposophy with this gentleman by relating it to his own field, to botany. I therefore spoke to him of, and out of, the nature of the plant, the nature of the blossom, of germination, gently inclining these various aspects of botany towards anthroposophy. He was not in the least interested. On the other hand he was interested—and very well versed here—in all accounts coming from the Theosophical Society about the etheric body, astral body and so forth. For heaven's sake, he was thinking, I have to lecture on botany and explain plants to my university students. If anthroposophy plays into this, it will be dire. That must not happen—I must protect this field and keep it pure of such things. I must be a proper professor, more or less like all the others. And for this reason he wasn't in the least interested when I started speaking about plants from an anthroposophic perspective, despite the fact that he is a botanist. On the other hand it was fine to speak at a great remove from science of the etheric body and astral body, and preferably also of kama manas and budhi manas and so forth. Root races and rounds were also a fine subject for him, since empirical research never touches on them.

The scholars of an older variety, you see, were not much interested in their science being imbued with anthroposophy. Younger friends came along, and with their more integrated soul nature felt a need for an encounter, an engagement between their science and anthroposophy. And here two sides emerged: one, if you will excuse me, the pack of hounds who fell upon anthroposophy, and the other our younger members who seek an encounter between anthroposophy and their science. In a perfectly natural way, therefore, from without, scientific discourse has arisen. And it was therefore no longer possible for me, at School courses[30] and conferences, to speak—well not in an unscientific way, but let us say 'ascientifically', or in other words at a remove from science. What approached us from the world itself endowed these institutions and enterprises with a kind of academic character, which was also necessitated by the fact that anthroposophy gradually had to intervene and engage in practical life, even, say, in medical therapy. All this came towards anthroposophy as a real demand from the world. As I said, if our older friends recognize that esotericism still does continue, and if they observe how anthroposophy can enter the current of science and make it fruitful, they may hopefully decide that what they hear at these conferences—about differential equations, integral numbers and so forth—is rather different from what they were used to but is nevertheless necessary.

The difficulty lies elsewhere really, not so much in these two streams which you can discern everywhere, and which may elicit somewhat ambivalent feelings in you. My dear friends, it is not so much these two streams I wished to speak of, but something of importance to me at present. In one's involvement in anthroposophic life today, one finds a continuation of old esotericism on the one hand and, on the other, exoteric, scientific endeavour. Between these two lies an abyss—there is no connection between them. And this is primarily what we should consider. In diverse fields we have very important, fine anthroposophic contributions, and on the other hand we have a continuation of the old esotericism. But we simply have too few people today, too few powers available, to build a bridge over this abyss between them. There are people who speak very well today about anthroposophy in the fields of botany, chemistry, physics and so on. And the old esotericism can also be perpetuated. But no bridge leads from one to the other, and this is why so many have become confused. It certainly is possible to build this bridge, and it must be built. But today, as yet, an abyss yawns between them, and the active workers amongst us are too few as yet to accomplish in *all* fields what needs to be accomplished. But these deficiencies—for that's what they are—are very much ignored and overlooked.

My dear friends, if we can develop a necessary seriousness of outlook, one that arises from the kinds of remarks I made at the beginning today, and from our observations yesterday and the day before, when we consider the very serious situation in which humanity finds itself today, we will say the following. However many deficiencies anthroposophy may have at present—and we must be fully aware of them—at the same time we should ensure that we have the patience to wait for enough active workers to fill in or at least bridge the gulf between our exoteric and esoteric endeavours.

Naturally, in our relationship with the world, a difficulty arises because whatever is accomplished at conferences always remains within them. You need only recall the really wonderful Stuttgart congress[31] which in itself ran magnificently and yet remained an internal affair. There was no talk of disseminating or publicizing the work accomplished there. No one is concerning themselves with this. And this has been true so far of every single enterprise. We have far too few active proponents to achieve here what needs to be achieved. It is because of this that people who sniff about in the anthroposophic movement for a moment or two, and maybe attend a lecture here or there—insufficient to form a judgement, and yet they do judge—pour forth their judgements of anthroposophy without knowing anything about it. This is partly because we have too few active workers and proponents, and partly because there is just too little seriousness of the kind I was referring to today.

You see, my dear friends, if the anthroposophic movement were to make a unified impression, the time would have arrived when we could have begun to strike a tone in the world, however quietly, that would show anthroposophy to be concerned with the most serious matters not just of our age but of the whole of our human future. What is published about anthroposophy in various journals has been written mostly in absolute ignorance, or also with malicious intent.

Someone has sent me a review[32] of my last lecture cycle in Germany[33] by an author I don't know. This was the cycle so appallingly disrupted,[34] as you have heard, by parties who are certainly attempting to eradicate anthroposophy in ever more insistent and deplorable ways. I have said repeatedly that these things will get worse and worse, and there's no need for me to reiterate that. But when such terrible things recur, I have noticed that people in the broadest circles, and even within our society, believe that nothing worse can happen and there's no need to be alarmed. Believe me, the worst has *not* yet happened!

But that isn't what I wished to say. Instead it is worth noting that here and there some people do have a subtle inkling of the importance of the impulses making themselves felt in our time. The author who wrote this critique has no sense whatever of the significance of what, for instance, I was saying yesterday: that we ought not to overlook the culture of rational thought that has been achieved in western civilization in recent centuries, and that therefore we cannot return to ancient Indian yogic breathing, nor should we seek in former, primitive epochs of humanity's evolution to find the powers for penetrating into the world of spirit. The writer of the review is very much one of those who believe that, since we have now gone beyond the pale of all true human dignity and humanity, there is no other option than to return to former paths by which humankind once entered worlds of spirit. This is the great error—that people are unable to find a path of schooling fitting for our immediate present, for the soul nature of today.

Well, the writer in question thinks I am making compromises when I keep saying that we must consider what is necessary in the modern world. This is why he writes:

> Steiner's personal vocation fails where—facing the huge complexity of Europe—he attempts practical compromises.

In fact it is no compromise, but something necessitated by the *inner* context of the situation! We can overlook here the way in which he formulates his terms. Well, I can't neatly summarize what he says, and so I will simply read the passage as it stands:

> The prophet must feel faint in the face of the obdurate nature of a 'ground of given realities'. But he ceases to be a 'prophet' of full potency where he becomes a spiritual politician, and makes corresponding concessions to these realities.

In fact no concessions are made. That is his great error here.

> The radiant power of all prophethood consists, after all, in its radicalism. The prophet—without resorting to small-brained, mundane political manoeuverings—must testify to the living spirit; must, as an insensible mediator, hurl the seed of mighty principles into humanity and remain untroubled by the times and seasons of their realization. He must leave this realization to the birthpangs of the populace itself.
>
> Anthroposophy is no longer alone in perceiving the need for the salvation of a Europe whose poor cosmic circulation is gradually bringing the whole planet to a standstill.

Well, at least we can see some small awareness here that there is 'poor circulation, and poor community with the cosmos' in modern European civilization.

> The objectified synthesis of all European philosophy emerges: the doctrine of the polarity of contrasts and its central resolution and balance—that of creative indifference. This signifies a revolution of our whole human perspective. We see the complex of humanity at the edge of a giddy abyss, completely at odds with universal power, filled with a one-sidedly differentiated energy, closed off from the whole cosmos: a cadaver with blocked arteries, a catastrophe in the solar system, a 'digestive disorder of God'. Here all insights merge: anthroposophy identifies itself with the doctrine of creative indifference; the mystery cults of the Egyptians are reawoken, and the breathing exercises of Indian yogis acquire new significance.

The writer now continues by expressing his view that, given this digestive disorder of modern civilization, these blocked vessels and constipation, the only option is to return to yogic practice. Nevertheless we can see that he does begin, albeit in a rather odd and inexpert, dilettantish way, to grasp the seriousness of the situation. He goes on:

> At night we switch off our consciousness—as long as we are not yet too troubled by the fact that we bar ourselves from cosmic renewal through individuality—. . .

Naturally he's got this completely wrong. We cannot *draw* any powers of renewal from sleep, least of all if we do not turn towards spirituality.

> . . . and imbibe the healing powers of the cosmos without the hindrance of isolated awareness.

This is simply not a true picture of what happens in sleep.

> The moment we isolate ourselves, our whole life becomes mere decline, a consumption of capital, the run-off of stored powers, nothing but a process of putrefaction. The consequence of all individuality (as bourgeois ideology means it) is thus inescapable: death. Nothing stands in the way of human immortality—today a utopian fantasy—but the human being's mistaken disposition for core equilibrium.

He shows no understanding of what is involved: that what he describes very abstractly as equilibrium is something we can grasp tangibly when we see how the astral and etheric bodies join together in the region of the human heart. That is the central point for true balance. This balance has cosmic significance. Today people talk round everything in the abstract and are unable to penetrate into tangible realities.

> Today anthroposophy is coming close to yoga practice.

No, it is not: it is cultivating a different practice.

> But however we may object to anthroposophy's dogmas, Steiner has accomplished extraordinary work in standing against the whole of monist-materialistic science, which is historically burdened merely, rather than historically oriented. Perhaps Rudolf Steiner will succeed is realizing yoga practice in the face of hard-bitten materialism and the arrogance of Europe.

Yoga practice is not our aim. But combating hard-bitten materialism and European arrogance is certainly going in the right direction—as suggested by this author, albeit in an unwholesome way.

> Reaching the limits of its viability, Europe will, out of organic necessity, inevitably turn to this primordial wisdom of the Indian yogis, and recognize the spiritual importance of the breath.

It would go very, very ill with Europe if it were to do this. But we can see, nevertheless, faint signs here of an awareness of the serious situation which humanity needs to acknowledge.

Now it is possible that anthroposophy will be brutally murdered before it is able to carry out what its inner nature would undoubtedly enable it to. But something important has emerged here. I am not just speaking of this newspaper article, whose author I don't know. It was sent to me by the people who organized that lecture cycle. As I said, quite apart from this article, we can see quiet signs that people are beginning to point to the whole seriousness of modern humanity's situation.

And I would say this: only through such understanding of the grave seriousness of our situation can an outlook arise that is fully equal to anthroposophy. We ought to endeavour to bring together the two streams, on the one hand esoteric, on the other exoteric and scientific, arising from the needs of our time. We should be aware that these things have developed as real necessities, and that a time will come—when in fact anthroposophy will *not* be murdered—when there will be sufficient strength and enough people working actively to bridge the gulf between these two streams. This is what I wished to offer today as an internal guideline for us, connected with observations as important as the ones I sought to present over these past few days.

I am not yet sure when we can have the next lecture. I will announce the date on my return from the Vienna Congress.[35] I do hope this congress will be very well attended. I haven't had an opportunity to find out who here will be able to take part, but hopefully the congress in Vienna will be something that can publicize the general anthroposophic movement more widely than has been the case with our other events. What happens at these conferences really should flow on, flow over into the whole anthroposophic movement, and from there should be spread further into the world. Otherwise the great efforts that are always made to organize such events more or less go to waste.

Part Three

CONTRAST BETWEEN EAST AND WEST

LECTURE 9

17 JUNE 1922

IT will be my task today to speak about an aspect of anthroposophy that has a close affinity with human nature. Tomorrow I will move on to say something about the West-East Congress in Vienna which has just ended.[36] Today I want to speak about various anthroposophic matters.

We human beings are initially connected to the world through our senses, and this is of course the case during our waking life, as is apparent to everyone. With our various senses we perceive diverse realms of life and, through our inner activity, draw on this to create our view of the world. I say this only in passing, and each person can trace further for himself the nature of his waking life and what is encompassed in it.

But as human beings we do not only lead waking lives in the world. We also sleep. And during sleep our I and soul being are outside the body and live in a realm, an environment, that is initially hidden from ordinary view.

Everything I am saying here applies to begin with to modern human beings, that is, to human soul life as this has developed since the fifteenth century—a point in time we have described as one of extraordinary importance for more recent human evolution.

Now we must ask this. How, when asleep, do we relate to a world that is closed to ordinary awareness? But in this particular evolutionary period in which we live now, we immediately encounter a problem when trying to describe this, unless we recognize that humanity has indeed evolved, and that its soul life has passed through the most diverse stages.

When we consider human soul life, we find that people in our supposedly civilized world today have to make all kinds of efforts to form ideas and concepts. Our view of former periods of humanity is often very superficial. We look back to times when there was no education of the kind necessary today. Very superficially we look back to ancient human culture as it developed in the Orient, which existed without people being educated from a young age as is the case nowadays. In Europe itself it is almost impossible today to gain any idea at all of how differently education was regarded in the Orient in ancient times when, however, such striking, lofty and moving cultural achievements as oriental literature arose, as the Vedas and everything contained in oriental wisdom. Today people judge every fruit of the human mind as the outcome of the education, teaching and upbringing a person receives from childhood on, and of what he then makes of this education in the further outward course of life. It becomes apparent that we have to be taught and educated because we ourselves have to formulate our own thoughts and ideas about life. We would be quite helpless today if we were not able to formulate our own thoughts about life. Actually we are not yet very far advanced in what I will call the art of creating thoughts. And in education, specifically, we have to ensure that people develop this art, and that through our own efforts we acquire the ability to reflect on the world.

The ground was laid for this in the Greek era. The first cultural life in Europe began in ancient Greece but was still in a certain respect influenced by the Orient. It therefore developed a form of education that only emphasized development of the powers of thinking in the very earliest stages. This Greek culture was still influenced by the oriental outlook which did not encourage human beings to make efforts in their thinking or, putting it trivially, to formulate their own thoughts about things.

In western culture people—with some justification—admire Socrates[37] as one of the first to encourage thinking for oneself. But it would be quite wrong to conclude from this, because Europe was compelled to develop thinking for oneself by one's own efforts, that the Orient was devoid of thought-life. The Orient had a magnificent life of thought, and the further we look back through oriental culture the more magnificent do we find this to be. If we look back as far as the times prior to the Vedas and Vedantic philosophy—for these, as I have often pointed out, were not the earliest stages of oriental culture, which were never recorded in writing—the life of thinking in the ancient Orient was of magnificent proportions. For the past two or three millennia this has all become decadent in the Orient itself, is declining and fading. Today an oriental admires what I will call the last vestiges of a once wonderful life of thought. But this thought-life was not like ours, where—and please excuse the materialistic expression, which is only intended as a picture—we have to perspire to produce it, have to make great exertions. Oriental thought-life was inspired—thoughts and their connected structure appeared to the oriental quite naturally. His world-view corresponded to the inspired thoughts he received. And he always had a sense that his thoughts came as a gift to him. The exertion, the inner exertion to compose and formulate thoughts, was something unknown to him. From the moment he awoke to the moment he fell asleep he felt thoughts came to him as gifts. His whole soul life was coloured accordingly by this; he was grateful to the gods because they gave him these thought-gifts. He felt the thoughts living in him, as a human being, were an influx of divine, spiritual powers. Thus people had a very different stance towards thoughts and thinking.

Ancient oriental thought-life was therefore not so distinct from feeling, from the heartfelt affairs of humankind, as is true today in the modern mind. It is precisely because people felt that thoughts were gifts that every thought they had seemed to raise them up as human beings: a religious feeling was connected with every thought. Human beings felt that they must meet the powers that granted them full thoughts with a kind of religious piety. They were less aware of separate, distinct thoughts than of the overall configuration of connected thoughts.

But what was the objective external cause of this outlook in oriental people? It was that in these more ancient times people slept differently from how we sleep today. As I and soul being we primarily depart from our head when we fall asleep. The primary organs of metabolism and our limbs are not separated so strongly from us. When a person sleeps, the soul and I still indwell the limbs and metabolism. We ought not to think that the I and soul abandon the whole us when we sleep, but that they primarily leave the head. I have often explained and described this, and I'd now like to depict it schematically again. Here we have the waking state [drawing, below, left] and here, in red, the I and the soul still penetrate the physical and etheric body. It would be wrong if I drew a sleeping person as the etheric and physical body remaining here in the bed, with the I and astral body or soul simply separate alongside them. I need to draw it like this: here [white] are the physical organs, the limbs—but the arms really belong here too; and only for the head will I draw the I and human soul outside of us, for when asleep, strictly speaking, we are separated from our physical body and etheric body only in the case of the head [red].

In the ancient times I was speaking of, it was true to say that during sleep the organs of the human head, thus primarily the neurosensory system and a part of the breathing system which

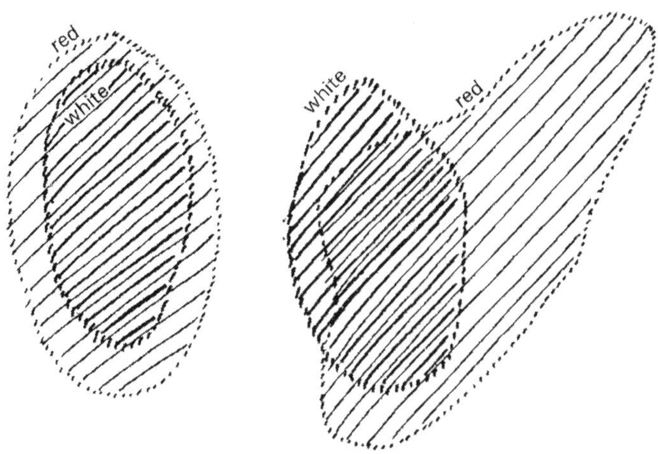

penetrates the head, were the arena where divine, spiritual beings connected with the earth unfolded their activities.

I am not speaking metaphorically when I point in earnest to realities by saying that in the most ancient periods of human evolution, divine, spiritual beings worked on earth in human beings during sleep and withdrew from them when they awoke. When people slept these beings took up dwelling in human heads. The human I and soul had departed from the head, and these divine, spiritual beings undertook their affairs there. When a person woke again in the morning, immersing himself in his head again, he found there the fruits remaining from the influence of the divine, spiritual beings who had been active in his head during sleep, organizing his nerve processes according to their laws, and exerting effects, right into the blood circulation, on the workings of the etheric and physical body. Apart from those schooled in the mysteries, the great majority of people were not clear that this was so, but they still experienced it. On awakening, therefore, a person found the deeds of the gods present in his head. And in his waking life, when he perceived the whole context of thoughts, this was because the gods had been active in his head during sleep. Every morning, we can say, the oriental came upon the legacy of what the gods had accomplished during his sleep as they undertook their affairs there. And he perceived this as thought Inspiration. It is not true to say therefore that divine, spiritual beings directly inspired these ancient people during waking life, but that they did so by going about their own business when these people were asleep. And everything that led to the social conduct of people in those ancient times was, basically, Inspiration. We must say that the divine, spiritual beings were at that time certainly able to arrange earthly affairs by eliciting, for instance, mutual trust among people through their sleep life, by implanting there the obedience which the great masses showed to their leaders. We really can say therefore that a collaboration between the divine, spiritual world and the earthly world existed in those ancient times in oriental culture. And this was only because the whole human organization was different in those days.

I have often mentioned that people today believe that human nature has always been as it is today, for as long as humankind has lived on earth: the same physical organism, the same soul nature, the same spiritual nature of the I. When modern historians write about ancient Egypt and try to decipher Egyptian texts, they think that although people in those days were not as clever as they are now, basically they thought, felt and acted as we do. If they look back far enough they believe that we were a kind of higher ape, passing on from this stage to—well, whatever the historians imagine. But when historical times began, their view is that people's thinking, feeling and will was as it is today, that their etheric and physical organization was the same too.

This isn't the case. Through history, also, human nature has changed markedly. You need only recall an aspect I mentioned previously:[38] that the Greeks saw their surroundings in a purely physical way. The Greeks did not yet see blue as we do, but rather a reddish tinge. And people today are actually wrong if they think the Greeks, since they had such a developed aesthetic sense, must have taken the same delight in the beauty of the blue sky as we do. The Greeks saw the warm, reddish, yellow colours, and scarcely distinguished green from blue. They therefore saw the sky very differently from how we ordinarily do today. Human eyes themselves have also become very different over the course of human evolution, even if only in subtler, more delicate ways. Our whole sensory organization has changed through history. And in those ancient oriental times I have been speaking of, our sensory organization was such that people were not distracted and prevented from dedicating themselves, on awakening, to the deeds of the gods that emerged from their organism, and were made available to them while they were asleep.

Gradually humanity's sensory organization bound him in so vivid a way to the external world that this immediately prevented him, when he awoke, from attending to what remained in him as the legacy of his sleep. Even if the gods were still to order their affairs in our head while we sleep—they no longer do so because of the change in human organization; this has no further importance for humanity's evolution—we would gain nothing at all from this for our further development. On the contrary, because the senses as they have now become are strongly engrossed in the external world when we awaken, we would be unable to pay attention to any such legacy from sleep; and therefore it would work back into the body instead of being assimilated into our awareness. People today would be unable to feel within them what the gods had done in the arena of their head organization while they were asleep, and working back into their organism this would make them age prematurely.

In more ancient times, what people experienced in sleep was assimilated by them in their waking life, and this was because their senses were not so oriented to the external world as is the case today. People could therefore live in union with the divine world. This life of theirs really was a communion with the world of the gods. One cannot see the gods with one's senses; because human senses were not yet so oriented to the external world as they are today, people in ancient times had the capacity to experience the deeds of the gods.

But then a later period arrived—more or less the millennium preceding the Mystery of Golgotha—when even in the oriental world human senses, especially the eyes, became more receptive to external impressions. Humankind gradually and increasingly acquired the sensory organization it would later possess, complementing this with what it inwardly retained of its nerve organization from ancient times, which still enabled it to experience divine, spiritual deeds. In older times human beings had still experienced divine, spiritual deeds in a pure form, without mingling sense impressions with this. Now, though they still experienced something since the gods had not departed from them altogether, this was immediately assimilated into their sensory organization. In a great proportion of humanity, therefore, a singular condition arose in which the gods, beings of spirit, were, if you like, fetched in to the human senses. I can put it like this: what had formerly been a pure, spiritual vision of divine, spiritual beings became a belief in ghosts.

Belief in ghosts did not originate in primordial humanity. Vision of divine, spiritual beings was present from the earliest times but the belief in ghosts arose when sense perception was mingled with this vision. As the mystery culture of the Orient came over to Europe and was, for example, assimilated into the wonderful cultural life of Greece in its art and philosophy, the perception of ghosts also arrived.

In this last millennium before the Mystery of Golgotha, a pure, oriental vision had begun to decline and came to be a kind of ghost perception in a great many people. A true spiritual vision transformed into sensory terms migrated to Europe as a belief in ghosts. We can say that this belief is a last gasp, the end of a lofty, albeit dreamy, spiritual vision, which once signified a great flowering of civilization at one stage in humanity's evolution.

What I have described here, as the sense ancient, oriental people had that their head in sleep was the earthly arena of the divine world, was something people ordinarily just felt. Someone initiated into the mysteries, however, knew that it was so. And the opposite of this is now emerging already in the rise of a new culture.

This new culture is still in its infancy, and is more pronounced the further west we come. It would have made no sense to the ancient oriental to say that human thoughts do not pulse through the human will. He knew that what lived in his will, even in his blood, was a gift from the gods. The gods gave him his thoughts, and unfolded a mighty strength in his sleeping state, which he experienced as Inspiration.

Today when we look to the East, to the last vestiges of what lives, say, in the philosophy of Soloviev,[39] there is something in him, particularly, that shows us he would not and could not understand if one were to say that thoughts have no power of impulse in us, they do not carry the will.

But that is very much the view of modern, western people, particularly in America. Americans demonstrate this in their view of physiology and biology. America's science, if we study its more intimate characteristics, is something very different from the science of Europe, not to mention the scholarship of the East.

Westerners describe how little importance thoughts have for the human will. And this is because they are so strongly aware of creating thoughts themselves. They cannot pick thoughts out of the blue. A modern American thinks that the thoughts a person assimilates pale in significance beside the family context, the political party, the fraternity or religion he has grown into through his social circumstances. All this has emotional traction for him, and it all determines his will. It isn't actually possible for him to determine the will through his thoughts. The will is determined by deep, subterranean sources of life such as family, party, country, religion and so forth. And the American, the westerner in general, thinks that thoughts do not hold dominion in him, but are only the prime minister, if you like, while the real ruler is the human organization, the will, drive, instinct. I have taken this from Carlyle:[40] thoughts are, by contrast, seen just as a valued minister, only the executive organ.

And we have to say that this is the view of great swathes of human beings who come storming to the attack upon old, outmoded traditions in the world. This is why there is such enthusiasm today for studying how primitive peoples lived: they are believed to have lived in drives and instincts, their thoughts being only a kind of mirror image of such instincts.

Westerners today look at human nature and see it to be driven by instincts. Why? Because, in these drives and instincts, human beings are not yet organized to perceive the spirit. They see only drive and instinct, with nothing spiritual behind it. Yet when a drive or instinct surfaces in us, even the coarsest instinct, there is spirit underlying it, even if this may sometimes be a very malign spirit. But people today are unable to grasp this spirit. The human race is certainly evolving, and we still have to progress towards the kind of spirituality which will enable us, when we look into ourselves and perceive our drives, instincts and desires, to perceive the spirit in them everywhere. This will come in future eventually. Here it makes no difference whether a person has good or evil instincts; evil spirits will be ahrimanic or luciferic ones, but they are still spiritual entities.

Saying that drives and instincts are the driving force within us is really on a par with the relationship between ghosts and spirituality in former times. You see, an ancient spirituality held sway in the oriental outlook [see drawing]. This developed and ultimately became, as I said, the belief in ghosts in the last millennium before the Mystery of Golgotha [see drawing, blue].

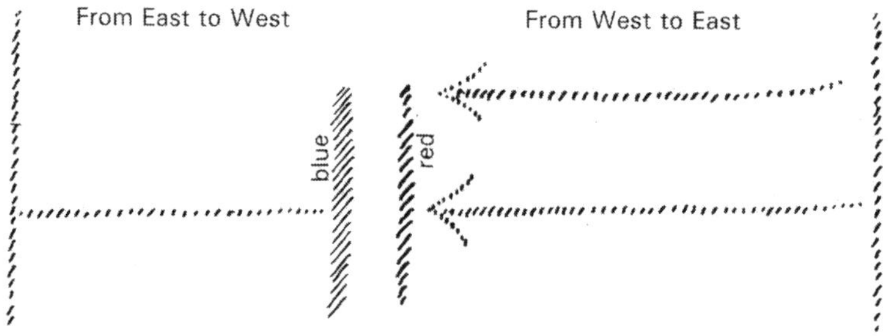

We have now reached a stage of world evolution where we can see how, on the one hand, the belief in ghosts emerged from an old spirituality; but at the same time, looking towards the future, a pure vision will eventually return. As yet a belief in ghosts still prevails, a kind of inner belief in ghosts. Just as someone who believes in ghosts thinks that they can be seen with our senses—that they appear as seen by us, so modern people in the West do not yet perceive spirituality when they look inwards, but instead the ghostly presences of drives, instincts and desires. These inner ghosts precede spirituality [red], whereas the old ghosts succeeded a former spirituality [blue]. And so we can say that from the East to the West an ancient pure spirituality evolved and gave rise over time to a belief in ghosts, the residues of which are still with us. From the West moving eastwards, approaching us and coming to realization in a far future, a later spirituality is developing, and is apparent in its early beginnings which are just as ghostlike as the old ghosts, and which now take the form of drives, instincts, desires and so on. Because of their outlook, modern academics inevitably assign drives, instincts and desires to humankind and look askance at the general belief in ghosts. They are unaware that this belief in ghosts is as well-founded and insightful as their own belief in desires, drives and instincts. They believe as much in the ghosts of the new beginning of spirituality as the general populace believes in the ghosts of its ending. And our European civilization has become so chaotic because the old ghosts have clashed in it with the new.

In an aphorism of the 'West-East Aphorisms',[41] published in this week's *Goetheanum*, I briefly characterized how modern humanity has been influenced for a long time now by the legacy of an ancient oriental spirituality on the one hand, internalized to become a belief in ghosts, and on the other by something only now beginning, germinating, that has not yet been released from the sensory nature of drives, instincts and desires. What people ordinarily call ghosts are spirits made sensory by the human organization. And drives, instincts and desires are a modern form of ghost; pointing us to the future, they have not yet attained spirituality.

The inner soul life of Europeans lives in this particular chaotic form of interplay between the old and the new ghosts, and we need a spiritual vision that can give us clarity about both. It is not just a matter of our outlook and world view, but these things are connected with our whole human life on earth. Inevitably this involves not just cultural and spiritual life, but also the life of law and rights, the state and economic life, since all of these of course proceed from our nature and constitution. But where does this whole evolution come from—that's something we must ask. The gods, as I said, the divine, spiritual beings, pursued their earthly concerns in the human head. In our threefold view of the human being, we distinguish the neurosensory aspect primarily in the head, the rhythmic part that lives in our centre, and the metabolism and limb aspect that is contained in the limbs and their inward continuation in us, the actual organs of metabolism [see drawing on p. 150]. We distinguish these three aspects in us, and thus we now know that the gods once ordered their earthly affairs by, as it were, setting up their workshop in the head of ancient human beings when they were asleep. What happens nowadays in our own case?

In us too the gods set up their workshop during sleep, no longer in the head, however, but in the organism of limbs and metabolism.

But the organism of limbs and metabolism—this is the important, significant thing—remains unconscious in us also when we're awake. As you will remember, I have often said that we are awake in our thoughts and ideas, but today, ordinarily, we do not know what happens after we think of lifting an arm or moving a hand so that the muscle actually accomplishes this intention. This whole action of our life of thought upon the organism remains veiled in obscurity in an unconscious realm even when we are awake. Thus the gods have their arena of activity on the earth today in a way that does not allow us, in the waking state, and in the natural course of development, to take up their legacy.

Today, divine, spiritual activity occurs in us during sleep, but our natural state does not enable us, when we awaken, to gain impressions of what the gods have done. In ancient times, the human organization was simply of a kind that led people to feel that thoughts inspired them. A modern person creates his thoughts, but divine-spiritual deeds do not yet work into this activity. This is something that must still evolve in humanity. And that is the task, the cosmic mission we can say, which spiritual science must set itself. It must bring the human being to such a stage of evolution, and education too must be included in this so that a person can perceive divine, spiritual deeds in full consciousness through his own resources. At the same time he will no longer see these inner ghosts of drives and instincts—and they really are as much ghosts in respect of our inner life as the outward apparitions that are called so. These outward ghosts are not mere fantasies either, but are divine-spiritual powers that people clothe in sense perceptions, in the process conceiving of them in an untrue, distorted form.

In the same way, the divine-spiritual powers at work in us are conceived in an untrue way when regarded as they are, as drives and instincts. People disparage ordinary ghosts, yet what they consider scientific is likewise nothing other than ghosts, simply inner ghosts. We must indeed pursue this transformation that cosmic evolution requires of us. Our whole culture must be penetrated by impulses of this nature. Herein lies the potential to emerge from forces of decline—or a chaotic interplay of forces of decline and resurgence, the latter a force which humanity today is still defending itself against—and, taking inspiration and impulse from the spirit, move towards possible future evolutionary stages of humanity. That is the important thing.

What I wished to offer you today is also a kind of East-West reflection, though of a more esoteric character. These East-West reflections are certainly of 'contemporary relevance' today—and I do not use the phrase in the trivial way that it so often is. Only by pursuing such reflections will humanity arrive at a certain awareness.

So we have to see that once upon a time, in ancient periods of earth's evolution, the human being in sleep—for he remains human in sleep when he does not outwardly carry his body around with him—also had a relationship with the gods that enabled him to perceive with eyes of soul, with eyes of spirit, the gods dwelling in his head. Later there remained only more or less the feeling echo of this when he awoke. Human beings increasingly departed from the divine-spiritual world, which they did however still perceive in a dreamlike fashion, looking back upon it after rising out of the body. That was at an earlier stage. Later they only perceived this world, as Inspiration, when they immersed themselves in the body again.

But as the gods have in a sense been drawn down further into our physical form, we have entered upon a relationship with them in which they seek out our organism of limbs and metabolism as their earthly workshop. This earthly arena, however, is one we do not entirely relinquish in sleep. And because we do not relinquish it fully, we will in turn be able to experience an impulse for our will from the world of the gods, for our social existence, but not in sleep. Instead we must experience it in our whole being also during waking life. This means that the human being must increasingly acquire conscious perceptions of the world of spirit. We must aim for this. That is what I wished to offer today in the context of West-East reflections. Tomorrow I will speak about my experience of this West-East Congress.[42]

NOTES

For the 2nd edition, 1998, the volume was reviewed and revised by Anna Maria Balastèr and Ulla Trapp. The new edition was expanded to include the second half of the lecture of 28 May 1922. Additions were made to the notes, and an index of names was added.

Source documents

All lectures were taken down in shorthand by the professional stenographer Helene Finckh, and printed from the typed transcripts, apart from the lecture of 28 May 1922, only the first half of which Finckh took down in shorthand. See note 28.

The titles

'Human Soul Life in Connection with World Evolution' was conceived by Rudolf Steiner.

The title 'Human Spiritual Striving in Connection with Earth Evolution' can be traced back to the first publication of the lectures in the Newsletter of 1928, and was probably given by Marie Steiner.

The title of the published (German) volume 'Human Soul Life and Spiritual Striving' originated with the editor of the first edition.

The board drawings

The original board drawings and captions for these lectures by Steiner have been preserved, since black paper was pinned to the board for this purpose. Reduced in size, they are reproduced in Volume IX in the series *Rudolf Steiner, Wandtafelzeichnungen zum Vortragswerk*. We retained the drawn copies of these illustrations inserted into the text in earlier editions.

1. Rose of Shiraz: a city in southern Iran, known for its cultivation of roses.
2. *Theosophy. Introduction to a Supersensible Knowledge of the World and Human Destiny*, GA 9.
3. Johann Friedrich Herbart, 1776–1842, philosopher and educator.
4. A reference to Goethe's *Faust, Part 1*, verses 1966–7.
5. Goethe, *Faust, Part 1*, verses 577f.
6. No source found for this.

7. Lloyd George, 1863–1945, British statesman, Prime Minister from 1916 to 1922.
8. Georges Clemenceau, 1841–1929, French statesman, Prime Minister 1906 to 1909, and 1917 to 1920.
9. Otto Prince of Bismarck, Duke of Lauenburg, 1815–98, Chancellor of the German Empire.
10. Goethe's *Faust, Part 1*, Prologue, verses 243ff.
11. GA 6, at the end of the chapter 'Personality and World View'.
12. 'One need not seek anything behind the phenomena, for they themselves are the teaching.' See *Goethes Naturwissenschaftliche Schriften*, edited with a commentary by Rudolf Steiner in Kürschner's *Deutsche National-Litteratur*, 5 vols, GA 1a–e, reprinted Dornach 1975, Vol. V, *Sprüche in Prosa*, p. 376.
13. Spectral analysis: method of proving the nature of substances (including those on planets) through the light spectrum, developed by Robert Wilhelm Bunsen (1811–99), German chemist, and Gustav Robert Kirchhoff (1824–87), German physicist.
14. Developed by Hans Driesch (1867–1941), German biologist. Chief work, *Philosophie des Organischen*, 2 vols, 1909.
15. Psychoid: concept in vitalism for soul-type entities, also used by C.J. Jung as a term for certain strata of the soul.
16. *The Theory of Knowledge Implicit in Goethe's World View, with Particular Reference to Schiller*, GA 2; *Truth and Science*, GA 3; *The Philosophy of Freedom*, GA 4.
17. Cf. for instance in *The Apocalypse of St John*, GA 104, Lecture 10, 27 June 1908.
18. GA 7 and 8.
19. Ernst Haeckel, 1834–1919, scientist. Founder of Monism, and proponent of Darwin's theory of evolution.
20. See note 18.
21. In the essay 'The Education of the Child in the Light of Anthroposophy' published 1907 in the journal *Lucifer-Gnosis*.
22. GA 9.
23. GA 13.
24. GA 10.
25. Greek verse form composed of six dactyls.
26. Five-foot verse form, composed of two dactyls, a hiatus and two further dactyls.
27. See for instance: *Anthroposophy, Psychosophy, Pneumatosophy*, 12 lectures, Berlin, 23 October 1909 to 16 December 1911, GA 115; also, *Beiträge zur Rudolf Steiner Gesamtausgabe*, nos 14 and 34.
28. The second part of the lecture was not in the first edition of the volume since the stenographer Helene Finckh did not include this section in the typescript based on her transcript. This was only done years later by Hedwig Frey and Güenther Frenz, after the quoted newspaper article was discovered.
29. The lecture cycle *The Orient in the Light of the Occident. The Children of Lucifer and the Brothers of Christ*, nine lectures given in Munich from 23 to 31 August 1909, GA 113, published under the title *The East in the Light of the West*. Steiner looked through the lectures before they were published in *Die Drei*, and added a preface.

30. School courses: The first anthroposophic School course took place in Dornach in September/October 1920. On this occasion Rudolf Steiner held lectures on *The Boundaries of Natural Science*, GA 322. The second course took place in April 1921, with Steiner's lectures 'The Fructifying Effect of Anthroposophy on Specialized Fields', GA 76. Further School courses were organized in Darmstadt in July 1921 (GA 77a), in Stuttgart in August/September 1921 (GA 78), in Berlin in March 1922 (GA 81) and The Hague in April 1922 (GA 82). The Vienna Congress with Steiner's lectures on *West and East, Contrasting Worlds* (GA 83) was held between 1 and 12 June 1922.
31. A general, public conference entitled 'Cultural Outlooks of the Anthroposophical Movement' took place at Gustav-Siegle House in Stuttgart from 28 August to 7 September 1921. Numerous anthroposophic speakers gave lectures on various fields, and Steiner gave a series of eight evening lectures on the theme of 'Anthroposophy, its Roots in Knowledge and its Practical Fruits, with an introduction on the adverse effects of agnosticism on true humanity', GA 78.
32. 'Anthroposophy and Yoga Practice', published in the *Berliner Börsen-Courier* no. 299, 17 May 1922.
33. During a lecture tour organized by Wolff and Sachs concert agency, from 12 to 22 May 1922, Rudolf Steiner spoke in Berlin, Breslau, Munich, Mannheim, Elberfeld, Cologne, Bremen, Hamburg and Leipzig on the theme of 'Anthroposophy and Spirit Knowledge', GA 78.
34. A lecture in Munich on 15 May 1922 was badly disrupted by right-wing radicals. See Hans Büchenbacher's report 'München 1922' in *Erinnerungen an Rudolf Steiner*, Stuttgart 1979. See also Thomas Meyer, *Milestones in the Life of Rudolf Steiner and in the Development of Anthroposophy*, Temple Lodge Publishing, 2015. There were also disturbances in Elberfeld, as Rudolf Steiner reported in a letter to Marie Steiner on 19 May 1922 (in GA 262).
35. West-East Congress in Vienna, held from 1 to 12 June 1922 as the second international congress of the anthroposophic movement. It represented a high-point of Steiner's public activity. See GA 83, *West and East, Contrasting Worlds*.
36. On 18 June 1922, Steiner gave a report to members about the Vienna Congress, extracts of which are published in GA 83.
37. Athenian philosopher, *c.* 470–399 BC.
38. For example, in the lecture on 31 December 1921 in Dornach (GA 209).
39. Vladimir Soloviev, 1835–1900, Russian philosopher.
40. Thomas Carlyle, 1795–1881, Scottish cultural philosopher and historian. We were unable to locate the statement by him that Steiner refers to here.
41. In *Der Goetheanum-Gedanke inmitten der Kulturkrisis der Gegenwart*. Collected essays 1921–5, GA 36.
42. See note 36.

RUDOLF STEINER'S COLLECTED WORKS

The German Edition of Rudolf Steiner's Collected Works (the *Gesamtausgabe* [GA] published by Rudolf Steiner Verlag, Dornach, Switzerland) presently runs to 354 titles, organized either by type of work (written or spoken), chronology, audience (public or other), or subject (education, art, etc.). For ease of comparison, the Collected Works in English [CW] follows the German organization exactly. A complete listing of the CWs follows with literal translations of the German titles. Other than in the case of the books published in his lifetime, titles were rarely given by Rudolf Steiner himself, and were often provided by the editors of the German editions. The titles in English are not necessarily the same as the German; and, indeed, over the past seventy-five years have frequently been different, with the same book sometimes appearing under different titles.

For ease of identification and to avoid confusion, we suggest that readers looking for a title should do so by CW number. Because the work of creating the Collected Works of Rudolf Steiner is an ongoing process, with new titles being published every year, we have not indicated in this listing which books are presently available. To find out what titles in the Collected Works are currently in print, please check our website at www.rudolfsteinerpress.com (or www.steinerbooks.org for US readers).

Written Work

CW 1	Goethe: Natural-Scientific Writings, Introduction, with Footnotes and Explanations in the text by Rudolf Steiner
CW 2	Outlines of an Epistemology of the Goethean World View, with Special Consideration of Schiller
CW 3	Truth and Science
CW 4	The Philosophy of Freedom
CW 4a	Documents to 'The Philosophy of Freedom'
CW 5	Friedrich Nietzsche, A Fighter against His Time
CW 6	Goethe's Worldview
CW 6a	Now in CW 30
CW 7	Mysticism at the Dawn of Modern Spiritual Life and Its Relationship with Modern Worldviews
CW 8	Christianity as Mystical Fact and the Mysteries of Antiquity
CW 9	Theosophy: An Introduction into Supersensible World Knowledge and Human Purpose
CW 10	How Does One Attain Knowledge of Higher Worlds?
CW 11	From the Akasha-Chronicle

CW 12	Levels of Higher Knowledge
CW 13	Occult Science in Outline
CW 14	Four Mystery Dramas
CW 15	The Spiritual Guidance of the Individual and Humanity
CW 16	A Way to Human Self-Knowledge: Eight Meditations
CW 17	The Threshold of the Spiritual World. Aphoristic Comments
CW 18	The Riddles of Philosophy in Their History, Presented as an Outline
CW 19	Contained in CW 24
CW 20	The Riddles of the Human Being: Articulated and Unarticulated in the Thinking, Views and Opinions of a Series of German and Austrian Personalities
CW 21	The Riddles of the Soul
CW 22	Goethe's Spiritual Nature And Its Revelation In 'Faust' and through the 'Fairy Tale of the Snake and the Lily'
CW 23	The Central Points of the Social Question in the Necessities of Life in the Present and the Future
CW 24	Essays Concerning the Threefold Division of the Social Organism and the Period 1915–1921
CW 25	Cosmology, Religion and Philosophy
CW 26	Anthroposophical Leading Thoughts
CW 27	Fundamentals for Expansion of the Art of Healing according to Spiritual-Scientific Insights
CW 28	The Course of My Life
CW 29	Collected Essays on Dramaturgy, 1889–1900
CW 30	Methodical Foundations of Anthroposophy: Collected Essays on Philosophy, Natural Science, Aesthetics and Psychology, 1884–1901
CW 31	Collected Essays on Culture and Current Events, 1887–1901
CW 32	Collected Essays on Literature, 1884–1902
CW 33	Biographies and Biographical Sketches, 1894–1905
CW 34	Lucifer-Gnosis: Foundational Essays on Anthroposophy and Reports from the Periodicals 'Lucifer' and 'Lucifer-Gnosis,' 1903–1908
CW 35	Philosophy and Anthroposophy: Collected Essays, 1904–1923
CW 36	The Goetheanum-Idea in the Middle of the Cultural Crisis of the Present: Collected Essays from the Periodical 'Das Goetheanum,' 1921–1925
CW 37	Now in CWs 260a and 251
CW 38	Letters, Vol. 1: 1881–1890
CW 39	Letters, Vol. 2: 1890–1925
CW 40	Truth-Wrought Words
CW 40a	Sayings, Poems and Mantras; Supplementary Volume
CW 42	Now in CWs 264–266
CW 43	Stage Adaptations
CW 44	On the Four Mystery Dramas. Sketches, Fragments and Paralipomena on the Four Mystery Dramas
CW 45	Anthroposophy: A Fragment from the Year 1910

Public Lectures

CW 51	On Philosophy, History and Literature
CW 52	Spiritual Teachings Concerning the Soul and Observation of the World
CW 53	The Origin and Goal of the Human Being
CW 54	The Riddles of the World and Anthroposophy
CW 55	Knowledge of the Supersensible in Our Times and Its Meaning for Life Today
CW 56	Knowledge of the Soul and of the Spirit
CW 57	Where and How Does One Find the Spirit?
CW 58	The Metamorphoses of the Soul Life. Paths of Soul Experiences: Part One
CW 59	The Metamorphoses of the Soul Life. Paths of Soul Experiences: Part Two
CW 60	The Answers of Spiritual Science to the Biggest Questions of Existence
CW 61	Human History in the Light of Spiritual Research
CW 62	Results of Spiritual Research
CW 63	Spiritual Science as a Treasure for Life
CW 64	Out of Destiny-Burdened Times
CW 65	Out of Central European Spiritual Life
CW 66	Spirit and Matter, Life and Death
CW 67	The Eternal in the Human Soul. Immortality and Freedom
CW 68	Public lectures in various cities, 1906–1918
CW 69	Public lectures in various cities, 1906–1918
CW 70	Public lectures in various cities, 1906–1918
CW 71	Public lectures in various cities, 1906–1918
CW 72	Freedom—Immortality—Social Life
CW 73	The Supplementing of the Modern Sciences through Anthroposophy
CW 73a	Specialized Fields of Knowledge and Anthroposophy
CW 74	The Philosophy of Thomas Aquinas
CW 75	Public lectures in various cities, 1906–1918
CW 76	The Fructifying Effect of Anthroposophy on Specialized Fields
CW 77a	The Task of Anthroposophy in Relation to Science and Life: The Darmstadt College Course
CW 77b	Art and Anthroposophy. The Goetheanum-Impulse
CW 78	Anthroposophy, Its Roots of Knowledge and Fruits for Life
CW 79	The Reality of the Higher Worlds
CW 80	Public lectures in various cities, 1922
CW 81	Renewal-Impulses for Culture and Science—Berlin College Course
CW 82	So that the Human Being Can Become a Complete Human Being
CW 83	Western and Eastern World-Contrast. Paths to Understanding It through Anthroposophy
CW 84	What Did the Goetheanum Intend and What Should Anthroposophy Do?

Lectures to the Members of the Anthroposophical Society

CW 88	Concerning the Astral World and Devachan
CW 89	Consciousness—Life—Form. Fundamental Principles of a Spiritual-Scientific Cosmology
CW 90	Participant Notes from the Lectures during the Years 1903–1905
CW 91	Participant Notes from the Lectures during the Years 1903–1905
CW 92	The Occult Truths of Ancient Myths and Sagas
CW 93	The Temple Legend and the Golden Legend
CW 93a	Fundamentals of Esotericism
CW 94	Cosmogony. Popular Occultism. The Gospel of John. The Theosophy in the Gospel of John
CW 95	At the Gates of Theosophy
CW 96	Origin-Impulses of Spiritual Science. Christian Esotericism in the Light of New Spirit-Knowledge
CW 97	The Christian Mystery
CW 98	Nature Beings and Spirit Beings—Their Effects in Our Visible World
CW 99	The Theosophy of the Rosicrucians
CW 100	Human Development and Christ-Knowledge
CW 101	Myths and Legends. Occult Signs and Symbols
CW 102	The Working into Human Beings by Spiritual Beings
CW 103	The Gospel of John
CW 104	The Apocalypse of John
CW 104a	From the Picture-Script of the Apocalypse of John
CW 105	Universe, Earth, the Human Being: Their Being and Development, as well as Their Reflection in the Connection between Egyptian Mythology and Modern Culture
CW 106	Egyptian Myths and Mysteries in Relation to the Active Spiritual Forces of the Present
CW 107	Spiritual-Scientific Knowledge of the Human Being
CW 108	Answering the Questions of Life and the World through Anthroposophy
CW 109	The Principle of Spiritual Economy in Connection with the Question of Reincarnation. An Aspect of the Spiritual Guidance of Humanity
CW 110	The Spiritual Hierarchies and Their Reflection in the Physical World. Zodiac, Planets and Cosmos
CW 111	Contained in CW 109
CW 112	The Gospel of John in Relation to the Three Other Gospels, Especially the Gospel of Luke
CW 113	The Orient in the Light of the Occident. The Children of Lucifer and the Brothers of Christ
CW 114	The Gospel of Luke
CW 115	Anthroposophy—Psychosophy—Pneumatosophy
CW 116	The Christ-Impulse and the Development of 'I'-Consciousness
CW 117	The Deeper Secrets of the Development of Humanity in Light of the Gospels

CW 118	The Event of the Christ-Appearance in the Etheric World
CW 119	Macrocosm and Microcosm. The Large World and the Small World. Soul-Questions, Life-Questions, Spirit-Questions
CW 120	The Revelation of Karma
CW 121	The Mission of Individual Folk-Souls in Connection with Germanic-Nordic Mythology
CW 122	The Secrets of the Biblical Creation-Story. The Six-Day Work in the First Book of Moses
CW 123	The Gospel of Matthew
CW 124	Excursus in the Area of the Gospel of Mark
CW 125	Paths and Goals of the Spiritual Human Being. Life Questions in the Light of Spiritual Science
CW 126	Occult History. Esoteric Observations of the Karmic Relationships of Personalities and Events of World History
CW 127	The Mission of the New Spiritual Revelation. The Christ-Event as the Middle-Point of Earth Evolution
CW 128	An Occult Physiology
CW 129	Wonders of the World, Trials of the Soul, and Revelations of the Spirit
CW 130	Esoteric Christianity and the Spiritual Guidance of Humanity
CW 131	From Jesus to Christ
CW 132	Evolution from the View Point of the Truth
CW 133	The Earthly and the Cosmic Human Being
CW 134	The World of the Senses and the World of the Spirit
CW 135	Reincarnation and Karma and their Meaning for the Culture of the Present
CW 136	The Spiritual Beings in Celestial Bodies and the Realms of Nature
CW 137	The Human Being in the Light of Occultism, Theosophy and Philosophy
CW 138	On Initiation. On Eternity and the Passing Moment. On the Light of the Spirit and the Darkness of Life
CW 139	The Gospel of Mark
CW 140	Occult Investigation into the Life between Death and New Birth. The Living Interaction between Life and Death
CW 141	Life between Death and New Birth in Relationship to Cosmic Facts
CW 142	The Bhagavad Gita and the Letters of Paul
CW 143	Experiences of the Supersensible. Three Paths of the Soul to Christ
CW 144	The Mysteries of the East and of Christianity
CW 145	What Significance Does Occult Development of the Human Being Have for the Sheaths—Physical Body, Etheric Body, Astral Body, and Self?
CW 146	The Occult Foundations of the Bhagavad Gita
CW 147	The Secrets of the Threshold
CW 148	Out of Research in the Akasha: The Fifth Gospel
CW 149	Christ and the Spiritual World. Concerning the Search for the Holy Grail

CW 150	The World of the Spirit and Its Extension into Physical Existence; The Influence of the Dead in the World of the Living
CW 151	Human Thought and Cosmic Thought
CW 152	Preliminary Stages to the Mystery of Golgotha
CW 153	The Inner Being of the Human Being and Life Between Death and New Birth
CW 154	How does One Gain an Understanding of the Spiritual World? The Flowing in of Spiritual Impulses from out of the World of the Deceased
CW 155	Christ and the Human Soul. Concerning the Meaning of Life. Theosophical Morality. Anthroposophy and Christianity
CW 156	Occult Reading and Occult Hearing
CW 157	Human Destinies and the Destiny of Peoples
CW 157a	The Formation of Destiny and the Life after Death
CW 158	The Connection Between the Human Being and the Elemental World. Kalevala—Olaf Åsteson—The Russian People—The World as the Result of the Influences of Equilibrium
CW 159	The Mystery of Death. The Nature and Significance of Middle Europe and the European Folk Spirits
CW 160	In CW 159
CW 161	Paths of Spiritual Knowledge and the Renewal of the Artistic Worldview
CW 162	Questions of Art and Life in Light of Spiritual Science
CW 163	Coincidence, Necessity and Providence. Imaginative Knowledge and the Processes after Death
CW 164	The Value of Thinking for a Knowledge That Satisfies the Human Being. The Relationship of Spiritual Science to Natural Science
CW 165	The Spiritual Unification of Humanity through the Christ-Impulse
CW 166	Necessity and Freedom in the Events of the World and in Human Action
CW 167	The Present and the Past in the Human Spirit
CW 168	The Connection between the Living and the Dead
CW 169	World-being and Selfhood
CW 170	The Riddle of the Human Being. The Spiritual Background of Human History. Cosmic and Human History, Vol. 1
CW 171	Inner Development-Impulses of Humanity. Goethe and the Crisis of the 19th Century. Cosmic and Human History, Vol. 2
CW 172	The Karma of the Vocation of the Human Being in Connection with Goethe's Life. Cosmic and Human History, Vol. 3
CW 173	Contemporary-Historical Considerations: The Karma of Untruthfulness, Part One. Cosmic and Human History, Vol. 4
CW 174	Contemporary-Historical Considerations: The Karma of Untruthfulness, Part Two. Cosmic and Human History, Vol. 5
CW 174a	Middle Europe between East and West. Cosmic and Human History, Vol. 6
CW 174b	The Spiritual Background of the First World War. Cosmic and Human History, Vol. 7

CW 175 Building Stones for an Understanding of the Mystery of Golgotha. Cosmic and Human Metamorphoses
CW 176 Truths of Evolution of the Individual and Humanity. The Karma of Materialism
CW 177 The Spiritual Background of the Outer World. The Fall of the Spirits of Darkness. Spiritual Beings and Their Effects, Vol. 1
CW 178 Individual Spiritual Beings and their Influence in the Soul of the Human Being. Spiritual Beings and their Effects, Vol. 2
CW 179 Spiritual Beings and Their Effects. Historical Necessity and Freedom. The Influences on Destiny from out of the World of the Dead. Spiritual Beings and Their Effects, Vol. 3
CW 180 Mystery Truths and Christmas Impulses. Ancient Myths and their Meaning. Spiritual Beings and Their Effects, Vol. 4
CW 181 Earthly Death and Cosmic Life. Anthroposophical Gifts for Life. Necessities of Consciousness for the Present and the Future.
CW 182 Death as Transformation of Life
CW 183 The Science of the Development of the Human Being
CW 184 The Polarity of Duration and Development in Human Life. The Cosmic Pre-History of Humanity
CW 185 Historical Symptomology
CW 185a Historical-Developmental Foundations for Forming a Social Judgement
CW 186 The Fundamental Social Demands of Our Time—In Changed Situations
CW 187 How Can Humanity Find the Christ Again? The Threefold Shadow-Existence of our Time and the New Christ-Light
CW 188 Goetheanism, a Transformation-Impulse and Resurrection-Thought. Science of the Human Being and Science of Sociology
CW 189 The Social Question as a Question of Consciousness. The Spiritual Background of the Social Question, Vol. 1
CW 190 Impulses of the Past and the Future in Social Occurrences. The Spiritual Background of the Social Question, Vol. 2
CW 191 Social Understanding from Spiritual-Scientific Cognition. The Spiritual Background of the Social Question, Vol. 3
CW 192 Spiritual-Scientific Treatment of Social and Pedagogical Questions
CW 193 The Inner Aspect of the Social Riddle. Luciferic Past and Ahrimanic Future
CW 194 The Mission of Michael. The Revelation of the Actual Mysteries of the Human Being
CW 195 Cosmic New Year and the New Year Idea
CW 196 Spiritual and Social Transformations in the Development of Humanity
CW 197 Polarities in the Development of Humanity: West and East Materialism and Mysticism Knowledge and Belief
CW 198 Healing Factors for the Social Organism
CW 199 Spiritual Science as Knowledge of the Foundational Impulses of Social Formation

CW 200 The New Spirituality and the Christ-Experience of the 20th Century

CW 201 The Correspondences Between Microcosm and Macrocosm. The Human Being—A Hieroglyph of the Universe. The Human Being in Relationship with the Cosmos: 1

CW 202 The Bridge between the World-Spirituality and the Physical Aspect of the Human Being. The Search for the New Isis, the Divine Sophia. The Human Being in Relationship with the Cosmos: 2

CW 203 The Responsibility of Human Beings for the Development of the World through their Spiritual Connection with the Planet Earth and the World of the Stars. The Human Being in Relationship with the Cosmos: 3

CW 204 Perspectives of the Development of Humanity. The Materialistic Knowledge-Impulse and the Task of Anthroposophy. The Human Being in Relationship with the Cosmos: 4

CW 205 Human Development, World-Soul, and World-Spirit. Part One: The Human Being as a Being of Body and Soul in Relationship to the World. The Human Being in Relationship with the Cosmos: 5

CW 206 Human Development, World-Soul, and World-Spirit. Part Two: The Human Being as a Spiritual Being in the Process of Historical Development. The Human Being in Relationship with the Cosmos: 6

CW 207 Anthroposophy as Cosmosophy. Part One: Characteristic Features of the Human Being in the Earthly and the Cosmic Realms. The Human Being in Relationship with the Cosmos: 7

CW 208 Anthroposophy as Cosmosophy. Part Two: The Forming of the Human Being as the Result of Cosmic Influence. The Human Being in Relationship with the Cosmos: 8

CW 209 Nordic and Central European Spiritual Impulses. The Festival of the Appearance of Christ. The Human Being in Relationship with the Cosmos: 9

CW 210 Old and New Methods of Initiation. Drama and Poetry in the Change of Consciousness in the Modern Age

CW 211 The Sun Mystery and the Mystery of Death and Resurrection. Exoteric and Esoteric Christianity

CW 212 Human Soul Life and Spiritual Striving in Connection with World and Earth Development

CW 213 Human Questions and World Answers

CW 214 The Mystery of the Trinity: The Human Being in Relationship with the Spiritual World in the Course of Time

CW 215 Philosophy, Cosmology, and Religion in Anthroposophy

CW 216 The Fundamental Impulses of the World-Historical Development of Humanity

CW 217 Spiritually Active Forces in the Coexistence of the Older and Younger Generations. Pedagogical Course for Youth

CW 217a	Youth's Cognitive Task
CW 218	Spiritual Connections in the Forming of the Human Organism
CW 219	The Relationship of the World of the Stars to the Human Being, and of the Human Being to the World of the Stars. The Spiritual Communion of Humanity
CW 220	Living Knowledge of Nature. Intellectual Fall and Spiritual Redemption
CW 221	Earth-Knowing and Heaven-Insight
CW 222	The Imparting of Impulses to World-Historical Events through Spiritual Powers
CW 223	The Cycle of the Year as Breathing Process of the Earth and the Four Great Festival-Seasons. Anthroposophy and the Human Heart (Gemüt)
CW 224	The Human Soul and its Connection with Divine-Spiritual Individualities. The Internalization of the Festivals of the Year
CW 225	Three Perspectives of Anthroposophy. Cultural Phenomena observed from a Spiritual-Scientific Perspective
CW 226	Human Being, Human Destiny, and World Development
CW 227	Initiation-Knowledge
CW 228	Science of Initiation and Knowledge of the Stars. The Human Being in the Past, the Present, and the Future from the Viewpoint of the Development of Consciousness
CW 229	The Experiencing of the Course of the Year in Four Cosmic Imaginations
CW 230	The Human Being as Harmony of the Creative, Building, and Formative World-Word
CW 231	The Supersensible Human Being, Understood Anthroposophically
CW 232	The Forming of the Mysteries
CW 233	World History Illuminated by Anthroposophy and as the Foundation for Knowledge of the Human Spirit
CW 233a	Mystery Sites of the Middle Ages: Rosicrucianism and the Modern Initiation-Principle. The Festival of Easter as Part of the History of the Mysteries of Humanity
CW 234	Anthroposophy. A Summary after 21 Years
CW 235	Esoteric Observations of Karmic Relationships in 6 Volumes, Vol. 1
CW 236	Esoteric Observations of Karmic Relationships in 6 Volumes, Vol. 2
CW 237	Esoteric Observations of Karmic Relationships in 6 Volumes, Vol. 3: The Karmic Relationships of the Anthroposophical Movement
CW 238	Esoteric Observations of Karmic Relationships in 6 Volumes, Vol. 4: The Spiritual Life of the Present in Relationship to the Anthroposophical Movement
CW 239	Esoteric Observations of Karmic Relationships in 6 Volumes, Vol. 5

CW 240	Esoteric Observations of Karmic Relationships in 6 Volumes, Vol. 6
CW 243	The Consciousness of the Initiate
CW 245	Instructions for an Esoteric Schooling
CW 250	The Building-Up of the Anthroposophical Society. From the Beginning to the Outbreak of the First World War
CW 251	The History of the Goetheanum Building-Association
CW 252	Life in the Anthroposophical Society from the First World War to the Burning of the First Goetheanum
CW 253	The Problems of Living Together in the Anthroposophical Society. On the Dornach Crisis of 1915. With Highlights on Swedenborg's Clairvoyance, the Views of Freudian Psychoanalysts, and the Concept of Love in Relation to Mysticism
CW 254	The Occult Movement in the 19th Century and Its Relationship to World Culture. Significant Points from the Exoteric Cultural Life around the Middle of the 19th Century
CW 255	Rudolf Steiner during the First World War
CW 255a	Anthroposophy and the Reformation of Society. On the History of the Threefold Movement
CW 255b	Anthroposophy and Its Opponents, 1919–1921
CW 256	How Can the Anthroposophical Movement Be Financed?
CW 256a	Futurum, Inc. / International Laboratories, Inc.
CW 256b	The Coming Day, Inc.
CW 257	Anthroposophical Community-Building
CW 258	The History of and Conditions for the Anthroposophical Movement in Relationship to the Anthroposophical Society. A Stimulus to Self-Contemplation
CW 259	The Year of Destiny 1923 in the History of the Anthroposophical Society. From the Burning of the Goetheanum to the Christmas Conference
CW 260	The Christmas Conference for the Founding of the General Anthroposophical Society
CW 260a	The Constitution of the General Anthroposophical Society and the School for Spiritual Science. The Rebuilding of the Goetheanum
CW 261	Our Dead. Addresses, Words of Remembrance, and Meditative Verses, 1906–1924
CW 262	Rudolf Steiner and Marie Steiner-von Sivers: Correspondence and Documents, 1901–1925
CW 263/1	Rudolf Steiner and Edith Maryon: Correspondence: Letters, Verses, Sketches, 1912–1924
CW 264	On the History and the Contents of the First Section of the Esoteric School from 1904 to 1914. Letters, Newsletters, Documents, Lectures
CW 265	On the History and from the Contents of the Ritual-Knowledge Section of the Esoteric School from 1904 to 1914. Documents, and Lectures from the Years 1906 to 1914, as well as on New Approaches to Ritual-Knowledge Work in the Years 1921–1924

CW 266/1	From the Contents of the Esoteric Lessons. Volume 1: 1904–1909. Notes from Memory of Participants. Meditation texts from the notes of Rudolf Steiner
CW 266/2	From the Contents of the Esoteric Lessons. Volume 2: 1910–1912. Notes from Memory of Participants
CW 266/3	From the Contents of the Esoteric Lessons. Volume 3: 1913, 1914 and 1920–1923. Notes from Memory of Participants. Meditation texts from the notes of Rudolf Steiner
CW 267	Soul-Exercises: Vol. 1: Exercises with Word and Image Meditations for the Methodological Development of Higher Powers of Knowledge, 1904–1924
CW 268	Soul-Exercises: Vol. 2: Mantric Verses, 1903–1925
CW 269	Ritual Texts for the Celebration of the Free Christian Religious Instruction. The Collected Verses for Teachers and Students of the Waldorf School
CW 270	Esoteric Instructions for the First Class of the School for Spiritual Science at the Goetheanum 1924, 4 Volumes
CW 271	Art and Knowledge of Art. Foundations of a New Aesthetic
CW 272	Spiritual-Scientific Commentary on Goethe's 'Faust' in Two Volumes. Vol. 1: Faust, the Striving Human Being
CW 273	Spiritual-Scientific Commentary on Goethe's 'Faust' in Two Volumes. Vol. 2: The Faust-Problem
CW 274	Addresses for the Christmas Plays from the Old Folk Traditions
CW 275	Art in the Light of Mystery-Wisdom
CW 276	The Artistic in Its Mission in the World. The Genius of Language. The World of Self-Revealing Radiant Appearances—Anthroposophy and Art. Anthroposophy and Poetry
CW 277	Eurythmy. The Revelation of the Speaking Soul
CW 277a	The Origin and Development of Eurythmy
CW 278	Eurythmy as Visible Song
CW 279	Eurythmy as Visible Speech
CW 280	The Method and Nature of Speech Formation
CW 281	The Art of Recitation and Declamation
CW 282	Speech Formation and Dramatic Art
CW 283	The Nature of Things Musical and the Experience of Tone in the Human Being
CW 284/285	Images of Occult Seals and Pillars. The Munich Congress of Whitsun 1907 and Its Consequences
CW 286	Paths to a New Style of Architecture. 'And the Building Becomes Human'
CW 287	The Building at Dornach as a Symbol of Historical Becoming and an Artistic Transformation Impulse
CW 288	Style-Forms in the Living Organic
CW 289	The Building-Idea of the Goetheanum: Lectures with Slides from the Years 1920–1921
CW 290	The Building-Idea of the Goetheanum: Lectures with Slides from the Years 1920–1921

CW 291	The Nature of Colours
CW 291a	Knowledge of Colours. Supplementary Volume to 'The Nature of Colours'
CW 292	Art History as Image of Inner Spiritual Impulses
CW 293	General Knowledge of the Human Being as the Foundation of Pedagogy
CW 294	The Art of Education, Methodology and Didactics
CW 295	The Art of Education: Seminar Discussions and Lectures on Lesson Planning
CW 296	The Question of Education as a Social Question
CW 297	The Idea and Practice of the Waldorf School
CW 297a	Education for Life: Self-Education and the Practice of Pedagogy
CW 298	Rudolf Steiner in the Waldorf School
CW 299	Spiritual-Scientific Observations on Speech
CW 300a	Conferences with the Teachers of the Free Waldorf School in Stuttgart, 1919 to 1924, in 3 Volumes, Vol. 1
CW 300b	Conferences with the Teachers of the Free Waldorf School in Stuttgart, 1919 to 1924, in 3 Volumes, Vol. 2
CW 300c	Conferences with the Teachers of the Free Waldorf School in Stuttgart, 1919 to 1924, in 3 Volumes, Vol. 3
CW 301	The Renewal of Pedagogical-Didactical Art through Spiritual Science
CW 302	Knowledge of the Human Being and the Forming of Class Lessons
CW 302a	Education and Teaching from a Knowledge of the Human Being
CW 303	The Healthy Development of the Human Being
CW 304	Methods of Education and Teaching Based on Anthroposophy
CW 304a	Anthroposophical Knowledge of the Human Being and Pedagogy
CW 305	The Soul-Spiritual Foundational Forces of the Art of Education. Spiritual Values in Education and Social Life
CW 306	Pedagogical Praxis from the Viewpoint of a Spiritual-Scientific Knowledge of the Human Being. The Education of the Child and Young Human Beings
CW 307	The Spiritual Life of the Present and Education
CW 308	The Method of Teaching and the Life-Requirements for Teaching
CW 309	Anthroposophical Pedagogy and Its Prerequisites
CW 310	The Pedagogical Value of a Knowledge of the Human Being and the Cultural Value of Pedagogy
CW 311	The Art of Education from an Understanding of the Being of Humanity
CW 312	Spiritual Science and Medicine
CW 313	Spiritual-Scientific Viewpoints on Therapy
CW 314	Physiology and Therapy Based on Spiritual Science
CW 315	Curative Eurythmy
CW 316	Meditative Observations and Instructions for a Deepening of the Art of Healing
CW 317	The Curative Education Course

CW 318 The Working Together of Doctors and Pastors
CW 319 Anthroposophical Knowledge of the Human Being and Medicine
CW 320 Spiritual-Scientific Impulses for the Development of Physics 1: The First Natural-Scientific Course: Light, Colour, Tone, Mass, Electricity, Magnetism
CW 321 Spiritual-Scientific Impulses for the Development of Physics 2: The Second Natural-Scientific Course: Warmth at the Border of Positive and Negative Materiality
CW 322 The Borders of the Knowledge of Nature
CW 323 The Relationship of the various Natural-Scientific Fields to Astronomy
CW 324 Nature Observation, Mathematics, and Scientific Experimentation and Results from the Viewpoint of Anthroposophy
CW 324a The Fourth Dimension in Mathematics and Reality
CW 325 Natural Science and the World-Historical Development of Humanity since Ancient Times
CW 326 The Moment of the Coming Into Being of Natural Science in World History and Its Development Since Then
CW 327 Spiritual-Scientific Foundations for Success in Farming. The Agricultural Course
CW 328 The Social Question
CW 329 The Liberation of the Human Being as the Foundation for a New Social Form
CW 330 The Renewal of the Social Organism
CW 331 Work-Council and Socialization
CW 332 The Alliance for Threefolding and the Total Reform of Society. The Council on Culture and the Liberation of the Spiritual Life
CW 332a The Social Future
CW 333 Freedom of Thought and Social Forces
CW 334 From the Unified State to the Threefold Social Organism
CW 335 The Crisis of the Present and the Path to Healthy Thinking
CW 336 The Great Questions of the Times and Anthroposophical Spiritual Knowledge
CW 337a Social Ideas, Social Reality, Social Practice, Vol. 1: Question-and-Answer Evenings and Study Evenings of the Alliance for the Threefold Social Organism in Stuttgart, 1919–1920
CW 337b Social Ideas, Social Realities, Social Practice, Vol. 2: Discussion Evenings of the Swiss Alliance for the Threefold Social Organism
CW 338 How Does One Work on Behalf of the Impulse for the Threefold Social Organism?
CW 339 Anthroposophy, Threefold Social Organism, and the Art of Public Speaking
CW 340 The National-Economics Course. The Tasks of a New Science of Economics, Volume 1
CW 341 The National-Economics Seminar. The Tasks of a New Science of Economics, Volume 2

CW 342	Lectures and Courses on Christian Religious Work, Vol. 1: Anthroposophical Foundations for a Renewed Christian Religious Working
CW 343	Lectures and Courses on Christian Religious Work, Vol. 2: Spiritual Knowledge—Religious Feeling—Cultic Doing
CW 344	Lectures and Courses on Christian Religious Work, Vol. 3: Lectures at the Founding of the Christian Community
CW 345	Lectures and Courses on Christian Religious Work, Vol. 4: Concerning the Nature of the Working Word
CW 346	Lectures and Courses on Christian Religious Work, Vol. 5: The Apocalypse and the Work of the Priest
CW 347	The Knowledge of the Nature of the Human Being According to Body, Soul and Spirit. On Earlier Conditions of the Earth
CW 348	On Health and Illness. Foundations of a Spiritual-Scientific Doctrine of the Senses
CW 349	On the Life of the Human Being and of the Earth. On the Nature of Christianity
CW 350	Rhythms in the Cosmos and in the Human Being. How Does One Come To See the Spiritual World?
CW 351	The Human Being and the World. The Influence of the Spirit in Nature. On the Nature of Bees
CW 352	Nature and the Human Being Observed Spiritual-Scientifically
CW 353	The History of Humanity and the World-Views of the Folk Cultures
CW 354	The Creation of the World and the Human Being. Life on Earth and the Influence of the Stars

SIGNIFICANT EVENTS IN THE LIFE OF RUDOLF STEINER

1829: June 23: birth of Johann Steiner (1829–1910)—Rudolf Steiner's father—in Geras, Lower Austria.

1834: May 8: birth of Franciska Blie (1834–1918)—Rudolf Steiner's mother—in Horn, Lower Austria. 'My father and mother were both children of the glorious Lower Austrian forest district north of the Danube.'

1860: May 16: marriage of Johann Steiner and Franciska Blie.

1861: February 25: birth of *Rudolf Joseph Lorenz Steiner* in Kraljevec, Croatia, near the border with Hungary, where Johann Steiner works as a telegrapher for the South Austria Railroad. Rudolf Steiner is baptized two days later, February 27, the date usually given as his birthday.

1862: Summer: the family moves to Mödling, Lower Austria.

1863: The family moves to Pottschach, Lower Austria, near the Styrian border, where Johann Steiner becomes stationmaster. 'The view stretched to the mountains ... majestic peaks in the distance and the sweet charm of nature in the immediate surroundings.'

1864: November 15: birth of Rudolf Steiner's sister, Leopoldine (d. November 1, 1927). She will become a seamstress and live with her parents for the rest of her life.

1866: July 28: birth of Rudolf Steiner's deaf-mute brother, Gustav (d. May 1, 1941).

1867: Rudolf Steiner enters the village school. Following a disagreement between his father and the schoolmaster, whose wife falsely accused the boy of causing a commotion, Rudolf Steiner is taken out of school and taught at home.

1868: A critical experience. Unknown to the family, an aunt dies in a distant town. Sitting in the station waiting room, Rudolf Steiner sees her 'form,' which speaks to him, asking for help. 'Beginning with this experience, a new soul life began in the boy, one in which not only the outer trees and mountains spoke to him, but also the worlds that lay behind them. From this moment on, the boy began to live with the spirits of nature ...'

1869: The family moves to the peaceful, rural village of Neudörfl, near Wiener-Neustadt in present-day Austria. Rudolf Steiner attends the village school. Because of the 'unorthodoxy' of his writing and spelling, he has to do 'extra lessons.'

1870: Through a book lent to him by his tutor, he discovers geometry: 'To grasp something purely in the spirit brought me inner happiness. I know that I first learned happiness through geometry.' The same tutor allows him to draw, while other students still struggle with their reading and writing. 'An artistic element' thus enters his education.

1871: Though his parents are not religious, Rudolf Steiner becomes a 'church child,' a favourite of the priest, who was 'an exceptional character.' 'Up to the age of ten or eleven, among those I came to know, he was far and away the most significant.' Among other things, he introduces Steiner to Copernican, heliocentric cosmology. As an altar boy, Rudolf Steiner serves at Masses, funerals, and Corpus Christi processions. At year's end, after an incident in which he escapes a thrashing, his father forbids him to go to church.

1872: Rudolf Steiner transfers to grammar school in Wiener-Neustadt, a five-mile walk from home, which must be done in all weathers.

1873–75: Through his teachers and on his own, Rudolf Steiner has many wonderful experiences with science and mathematics. Outside school, he teaches himself analytic geometry, trigonometry, differential equations, and calculus.

1876: Rudolf Steiner begins tutoring other students. He learns bookbinding from his father. He also teaches himself stenography.

1877: Rudolf Steiner discovers Kant's *Critique of Pure Reason*, which he reads and rereads. He also discovers and reads von Rotteck's *World History*.

1878: He studies extensively in contemporary psychology and philosophy.

1879: Rudolf Steiner graduates from high school with honours. His father is transferred to Inzersdorf, near Vienna. He uses his first visit to Vienna 'to purchase a great number of philosophy books'—Kant, Fichte, Schelling, and Hegel, as well as numerous histories of philosophy. His aim: to find a path from the 'I' to nature.

October 1879–1883: Rudolf Steiner attends the Technical College in Vienna—to study mathematics, chemistry, physics, mineralogy, botany, zoology, biology, geology, and mechanics—with a scholarship. He also attends lectures in history and literature, while avidly reading philosophy on his own. His two favourite professors are Karl Julius Schröer (German language and literature) and Edmund Reitlinger (physics). He also audits lectures by Robert Zimmermann on aesthetics and Franz Brentano on philosophy. During this year he begins his friendship with Moritz Zitter (1861–1921), who will help support him financially when he is in Berlin.

1880: Rudolf Steiner attends lectures on Schiller and Goethe by Karl Julius Schröer, who becomes his mentor. Also 'through a remarkable combination of circumstances,' he meets Felix Koguzki, a 'herb gatherer' and healer, who could 'see deeply into the secrets of nature.' Rudolf Steiner will meet and study with this 'emissary of the Master' throughout his time in Vienna.

1881: January: '... I didn't sleep a wink. I was busy with philosophical problems until about 12:30 a.m. Then, finally, I threw myself down on my couch. All my striving during the previous year had been to research whether the following statement by Schelling was true or not: *Within everyone dwells a secret, marvelous capacity to draw back from the stream of time—out of the self clothed in all that comes to us from outside—into our innermost being and there, in the immutable form of the Eternal, to look into ourselves*. I believe, and I am still quite certain of it, that I discovered this capacity in myself; I had long had an inkling of it. Now the whole of idealist philosophy stood before me in modified form. What's a sleepless night compared to that!'

Rudolf Steiner begins communicating with leading thinkers of the day, who send him books in return, which he reads eagerly.

July: 'I am not one of those who dives into the day like an animal in human form. I pursue a quite specific goal, an idealistic aim—knowledge of the truth! This cannot be done offhandedly. It requires the greatest striving in the world, free of all egotism, and equally of all resignation.'

August: Steiner puts down on paper for the first time thoughts for a 'Philosophy of Freedom.' 'The striving for the absolute: this human yearning is freedom.' He also seeks to outline a 'peasant philosophy,' describing what the worldview of a 'peasant'—one who lives close to the earth and the old ways—really is.

1881–1882: Felix Koguzki, the herb gatherer, reveals himself to be the envoy of another, higher initiatory personality, who instructs Rudolf Steiner to penetrate Fichte's philosophy and to master modern scientific thinking as a preparation for right entry into the spirit. This 'Master' also teaches him the double (evolutionary and involutionary) nature of time.

1882: Through the offices of Karl Julius Schröer, Rudolf Steiner is asked by Joseph Kürschner to edit Goethe's scientific works for the *Deutschen National-Literatur* edition. He writes 'A Possible Critique of Atomistic Concepts' and sends it to Friedrich Theodor Vischer.

1883: Rudolf Steiner completes his college studies and begins work on the Goethe project.

1884: First volume of Goethe's *Scientific Writings* (CW 1) appears (March). He lectures on Goethe and Lessing, and Goethe's approach to science. In July, he enters the household of Ladislaus and Pauline Specht as tutor to the four Specht boys. He will live there until 1890. At this time, he meets Josef Breuer (1842–1925), the co-author with Sigmund Freud of *Studies in Hysteria*, who is the Specht family doctor.

1885: While continuing to edit Goethe's writings, Rudolf Steiner reads deeply in contemporary philosophy (Eduard von Hartmann, Johannes Volkelt, and Richard Wahle, among others).

1886: May: Rudolf Steiner sends Kürschner the manuscript of *Outlines of Goethe's Theory of Knowledge* (CW 2), which appears in October, and which he sends out widely. He also meets the poet Marie Eugenie Delle Grazie and writes 'Nature and Our Ideals' for her. He attends her salon, where he meets many priests, theologians, and philosophers, who will become his friends. Meanwhile, the director of the Goethe Archive in Weimar requests his collaboration with the *Sophien* edition of Goethe's works, particularly the writings on colour.

1887: At the beginning of the year, Rudolf Steiner is very sick. As the year progresses and his health improves, he becomes increasingly 'a man of letters,' lecturing, writing essays, and taking part in Austrian cultural life. In August–September, the second volume of Goethe's *Scientific Writings* appears.

1888: January–July: Rudolf Steiner assumes editorship of the 'German Weekly' (*Deutsche Wochenschrift*). He begins lecturing more intensively, giving, for example, a lecture titled 'Goethe as Father of a New Aesthetics.' He meets and becomes soul friends with Friedrich Eckstein (1861–1939), a vegetarian, philosopher of symbolism, alchemist, and musician, who will introduce him to various spiritual currents (including Theosophy) and with whom he will meditate and interpret esoteric and alchemical texts.

1889: Rudolf Steiner first reads Nietzsche (*Beyond Good and Evil*). He encounters Theosophy again and learns of Madame Blavatsky in the Theosophical circle around Marie Lang (1858–1934). Here he also meets well-known figures of Austrian life, as well as esoteric figures like the occultist Franz Hartmann and Karl Leinigen-Billigen (translator of C.G. Harrison's *The Transcendental Universe*). During this period, Steiner first reads A.P. Sinnett's *Esoteric Buddhism* and Mabel Collins's *Light on the Path*. He also begins travelling, visiting Budapest, Weimar, and Berlin (where he meets philosopher Eduard von Hartmann).

1890: Rudolf Steiner finishes volume 3 of Goethe's scientific writings. He begins his doctoral dissertation, which will become *Truth and Science* (CW 3). He also meets the poet and feminist Rosa Mayreder (1858–1938), with whom he can exchange his most intimate thoughts. In September, Rudolf Steiner moves to Weimar to work in the Goethe-Schiller Archive.

1891: Volume 3 of the Kürschner edition of Goethe appears. Meanwhile, Rudolf Steiner edits Goethe's studies in mineralogy and scientific writings for the *Sophien* edition. He meets Ludwig Laistner of the Cotta Publishing Company, who asks for a book on the basic question of metaphysics. From this will result, ultimately, *The Philosophy of Freedom* (CW 4), which will be published not by Cotta but by Emil Felber. In October, Rudolf Steiner takes the oral exam for a doctorate in philosophy, mathematics, and mechanics at Rostock University, receiving his doctorate on the twenty-sixth. In November, he gives his first lecture on Goethe's 'Fairy Tale' in Vienna.

1892: Rudolf Steiner continues work at the Goethe-Schiller Archive and on his *Philosophy of Freedom*. *Truth and Science*, his doctoral dissertation, is published. Steiner undertakes to write introductions to books on Schopenhauer and Jean Paul for Cotta. At year's end, he finds lodging with Anna Eunike, née Schulz (1853–1911), a widow with four daughters and a son. He also develops a friendship with Otto Erich Hartleben (1864–1905) with whom he shares literary interests.

1893: Rudolf Steiner begins his habit of producing many reviews and articles. In March, he gives a lecture titled 'Hypnotism, with Reference to Spiritism.' In September, volume 4 of the Kürschner edition is completed. In November, *The Philosophy of Freedom* appears. This year, too, he meets John Henry Mackay (1864–1933), the anarchist, and Max Stirner, a scholar and biographer.

1894: Rudolf Steiner meets Elisabeth Förster Nietzsche, the philosopher's sister, and begins to read Nietzsche in earnest, beginning with the as yet unpublished *Antichrist*. He also meets Ernst Haeckel (1834–1919). In the fall, he begins to write *Nietzsche, A Fighter against His Time* (CW 5).

1895: May, *Nietzsche, A Fighter against His Time* appears.

1896: January 22: Rudolf Steiner sees Friedrich Nietzsche for the first and only time. Moves between the Nietzsche and the Goethe-Schiller Archives, where he completes his work before year's end. He falls out with Elisabeth Förster Nietzsche, thus ending his association with the Nietzsche Archive.

1897: Rudolf Steiner finishes the manuscript of *Goethe's Worldview* (CW 6). He moves to Berlin with Anna Eunike and begins editorship of the *Magazin für Literatur*. From now on, Steiner will write countless reviews, literary and philosophical articles, and so on. He begins lecturing at the 'Free Literary Society.' In September, he attends the Zionist Congress in Basel. He sides with Dreyfus in the Dreyfus affair.

1898: Rudolf Steiner is very active as an editor in the political, artistic, and theatrical life of Berlin. He becomes friendly with John Henry Mackay and poet Ludwig Jacobowski (1868–1900). He joins Jacobowski's circle of writers, artists, and scientists—'The Coming Ones' (*Die Kommenden*)—and contributes lectures to the group until 1903. He also lectures at the 'League for College Pedagogy.' He writes an article for Goethe's sesquicentennial, 'Goethe's Secret Revelation,' on the 'Fairy Tale of the Green Snake and the Beautiful Lily.'

1898–99: 'This was a trying time for my soul as I looked at Christianity. . . . I was able to progress only by contemplating, by means of spiritual perception, the evolution of Christianity. . . . Conscious knowledge of real Christianity began to dawn in me around the turn of the century. This seed continued to develop. My soul trial occurred shortly before the beginning of the twentieth century. It was decisive for my soul's development that I stood spiritually before the Mystery of Golgotha in a deep and solemn celebration of knowledge.'

1899: Rudolf Steiner begins teaching and giving lectures and lecture cycles at the Workers' College, founded by Wilhelm Liebknecht (1826–1900). He will continue to do so until 1904. Writes: *Literature and Spiritual Life in the Nineteenth Century; Individualism in Philosophy*; *Haeckel and His Opponents; Poetry in the Present;* and begins what will become (fifteen years later) *The Riddles of Philosophy* (CW 18). He also meets many artists and writers, including Käthe Kollwitz, Stefan Zweig, and Rainer Maria Rilke. On October 31, he marries Anna Eunike.

1900: 'I thought that the turn of the century must bring humanity a new light. It seemed to me that the separation of human thinking and willing from the spirit had peaked. A turn or reversal of direction in human evolution seemed to me a necessity.' Rudolf Steiner finishes *World and Life Views in the Nineteenth Century* (the second part of what will become *The Riddles of Philosophy*) and dedicates it to Ernst Haeckel. It is published in March. He continues lecturing at *Die Kommenden*, whose leadership he assumes after the death of Jacobowski. Also, he gives the Gutenberg Jubilee lecture before 7,000 typesetters and printers. In September, Rudolf Steiner is invited by Count and Countess Brockdorff to lecture in the Theosophical Library. His first lecture is on Nietzsche. His second lecture is titled 'Goethe's Secret Revelation.' October 6, he begins a lecture cycle on the mystics that will become *Mystics after Modernism* (CW 7). November-December: 'Marie von Sivers appears in the audience....' Also in November, Steiner gives his first lecture at the Giordano Bruno Bund (where he will continue to lecture until May, 1905). He speaks on Bruno and modern Rome, focusing on the importance of the philosophy of Thomas Aquinas as monism.

1901: In continual financial straits, Rudolf Steiner's early friends Moritz Zitter and Rosa Mayreder help support him. In October, he begins the lecture cycle *Christianity as Mystical Fact* (CW 8) at the Theosophical Library. In November, he gives his first 'Theosophical lecture' on Goethe's 'Fairy Tale' in Hamburg at the invitation of Wilhelm Hubbe-Schleiden. He also attends a gathering to celebrate the founding of the Theosophical Society at Count and Countess Brockdorff's. He gives a lecture cycle, 'From Buddha to Christ,' for the circle of the *Kommenden*. November 17, Marie von Sivers asks Rudolf Steiner if Theosophy needs a Western-Christian spiritual movement (to complement Theosophy's Eastern emphasis). 'The question was posed. Now, following spiritual laws, I could begin to give an answer....' In December, Rudolf Steiner writes his first article for a Theosophical publication. At year's end, the Brockdorffs and possibly Wilhelm Hubbe-Schleiden ask Rudolf Steiner to join the Theosophical Society and undertake the leadership of the German section. Rudolf Steiner agrees, on the condition that Marie von Sivers (then in Italy) work with him.

1902: Beginning in January, Rudolf Steiner attends the opening of the Workers' School in Spandau with Rosa Luxemberg (1870–1919). January 17, Rudolf Steiner joins the Theosophical Society. In April, he is asked to become general secretary of the German Section of the Theosophical Society, and works on preparations for its founding. In July, he visits London for a Theosophical congress. He meets Bertram Keightly, G.R.S. Mead, A.P. Sinnett, and Annie Besant, among others. In September, *Christianity as Mystical Fact* appears. In October, Rudolf Steiner gives his first public lecture on Theosophy ('Monism and Theosophy') to about three hundred people at the Giordano Bruno Bund. On October 19–21, the German Section of the Theosophical Society has its first meeting; Rudolf Steiner is the general secretary, and Annie Besant attends. Steiner lectures on practical karma studies. On October 23, Annie Besant inducts Rudolf Steiner into the Esoteric School of the Theosophical Society. On October 25, Steiner begins a weekly series of lectures: 'The Field of Theosophy.' During this year, Rudolf Steiner also first meets Ita Wegman (1876–1943), who will become his close collaborator in his final years.

1903: Rudolf Steiner holds about 300 lectures and seminars. In May, the first issue of the periodical *Luzifer* appears. In June, Rudolf Steiner visits

London for the first meeting of the Federation of the European Sections of the Theosophical Society, where he meets Colonel Olcott. He begins to write *Theosophy* (CW 9).

1904: Rudolf Steiner continues lecturing at the Workers' College and elsewhere (about 90 lectures), while lecturing intensively all over Germany among Theosophists (about 140 lectures). In February, he meets Carl Unger (1878–1929), who will become a member of the board of the Anthroposophical Society (1913). In March, he meets Michael Bauer (1871–1929), a Christian mystic, who will also be on the board. In May, *Theosophy* appears, with the dedication: 'To the spirit of Giordano Bruno.' Rudolf Steiner and Marie von Sivers visit London for meetings with Annie Besant. June: Rudolf Steiner and Marie von Sivers attend the meeting of the Federation of European Sections of the Theosophical Society in Amsterdam. In July, Steiner begins the articles in *Luzifer-Gnosis* that will become *How to Know Higher Worlds* (CW 10) and *Cosmic Memory* (CW 11). In September, Annie Besant visits Germany. In December, Steiner lectures on Freemasonry. He mentions the High Grade Masonry derived from John Yarker and represented by Theodore Reuss and Karl Kellner as a blank slate 'into which a good image could be placed.'

1905: This year, Steiner ends his non-Theosophical lecturing activity. Supported by Marie von Sivers, his Theosophical lecturing—both in public and in the Theosophical Society—increases significantly: 'The German Theosophical Movement is of exceptional importance.' Steiner recommends reading, among others, Fichte, Jacob Boehme, and Angelus Silesius. He begins to introduce Christian themes into Theosophy. He also begins to work with doctors (Felix Peipers and Ludwig Noll). In July, he is in London for the Federation of European Sections, where he attends a lecture by Annie Besant: 'I have seldom seen Mrs. Besant speak in so inward and heartfelt a manner. . . .' 'Through Mrs. Besant I have found the way to H.P. Blavatsky.' September to October, he gives a course of thirty-one lectures for a small group of esoteric students. In October, the annual meeting of the German Section of the Theosophical Society, which still remains very small, takes place. Rudolf Steiner reports membership has risen from 121 to 377 members. In November, seeking to establish esoteric 'continuity,' Rudolf Steiner and Marie von Sivers participate in a 'Memphis-Misraim' Masonic ceremony. They pay forty-five marks for membership. 'Yesterday, you saw how little remains of former esoteric institutions.' 'We are dealing only with a "framework". . . for the present, nothing lies behind it. The occult powers have completely withdrawn.'

1906: Expansion of Theosophical work. Rudolf Steiner gives about 245 lectures, only 44 of which take place in Berlin. Cycles are given in Paris, Leipzig, Stuttgart, and Munich. Esoteric work also intensifies. Rudolf Steiner begins writing *An Outline of Esoteric Science* (CW 13). In January, Rudolf Steiner receives permission (a patent) from the Great Orient of the Scottish A & A Thirty-Three Degree Rite of the Order of the Ancient

Freemasons of the Memphis-Misraim Rite to direct a chapter under the name 'Mystica Aeterna.' This will become the 'Cognitive-Ritual Section' (also called 'Misraim Service') of the Esoteric School. (See: *Freemasonry and Ritual Work: The Misraim Service*, CW 265). During this time, Steiner also meets Albert Schweitzer. In May, he is in Paris, where he visits Edouard Schuré. Many Russians attend his lectures (including Konstantin Balmont, Dimitri Mereszkovski, Zinaida Hippius, and Maximilian Woloshin). He attends the General Meeting of the European Federation of the Theosophical Society, at which Col. Olcott is present for the last time. He spends the year's end in Venice and Rome, where he writes and works on his translation of H.P. Blavatsky's *Key to Theosophy*.

1907: Further expansion of the German Theosophical Movement according to the Rosicrucian directive to 'introduce spirit into the world'—in education, in social questions, in art, and in science. In February, Col. Olcott dies in Adyar. Before he dies, Olcott indicates that 'the Masters' wish Annie Besant to succeed him: much politicking ensues. Rudolf Steiner supports Besant's candidacy. April-May: preparations for the Congress of the Federation of European Sections of the Theosophical Society—the great, watershed Whitsun 'Munich Congress,' attended by Annie Besant and others. Steiner decides to separate Eastern and Western (Christian-Rosicrucian) esoteric schools. He takes his esoteric school out of the Theosophical Society (Besant and Rudolf Steiner are 'in harmony' on this). Steiner makes his first lecture tours to Austria and Hungary. That summer, he is in Italy. In September, he visits Edouard Schuré, who will write the introduction to the French edition of *Christianity as Mystical Fact* in Barr, Alsace. Rudolf Steiner writes the autobiographical statement known as the 'Barr Document.' In *Luzifer-Gnosis*, 'The Education of the Child' appears.

1908: The movement grows (membership: 1,150). Lecturing expands. Steiner makes his first extended lecture tour to Holland and Scandinavia, as well as visits to Naples and Sicily. Themes: St. John's Gospel, the Apocalypse, Egypt, science, philosophy, and logic. *Luzifer-Gnosis* ceases publication. In Berlin, Marie von Sivers (with Johanna Mücke (1864–1949) forms the *Philosophisch-Theosophisch* (after 1915 *Philosophisch-Anthroposophisch*) *Verlag* to publish Steiner's work. Steiner gives lecture cycles titled *The Gospel of St. John* (CW 103) and *The Apocalypse* (104).

1909: *An Outline of Esoteric Science* appears. Lecturing and travel continues. Rudolf Steiner's spiritual research expands to include the polarity of Lucifer and Ahriman; the work of great individualities in history; the Maitreya Buddha and the Bodhisattvas; spiritual economy (CW 109); the work of the spiritual hierarchies in heaven and on earth (CW 110). He also deepens and intensifies his research into the Gospels, giving lectures on the Gospel of St. Luke (CW 114) with the first mention of two Jesus children. Meets and becomes friends with Christian Morgenstern (1871–1914). In April, he lays the foundation stone for the Malsch model—the building that will lead to the first Goetheanum. In May, the International Congress of the Federation of European Sections of the

Theosophical Society takes place in Budapest. Rudolf Steiner receives the Subba Row medal for *How to Know Higher Worlds*. During this time, Charles W. Leadbeater discovers Jiddu Krishnamurti (1895–1986) and proclaims him the future 'world teacher,' the bearer of the Maitreya Buddha and the 'reappearing Christ.' In October, Steiner delivers seminal lectures on 'anthroposophy,' which he will try, unsuccessfully, to rework over the next years into the unfinished work, *Anthroposophy (A Fragment)* (CW 45).

1910: New themes: *The Reappearance of Christ in the Etheric* (CW 118); *The Fifth Gospel; The Mission of Folk Souls* (CW 121); *Occult History* (CW 126); the evolving development of etheric cognitive capacities. Rudolf Steiner continues his Gospel research with *The Gospel of St. Matthew* (CW 123). In January, his father dies. In April, he takes a month-long trip to Italy, including Rome, Monte Cassino, and Sicily. He also visits Scandinavia again. July–August, he writes the first mystery drama, *The Portal of Initiation* (CW 14). In November, he gives 'psychosophy' lectures. In December, he submits 'On the Psychological Foundations and Epistemological Framework of Theosophy' to the International Philosophical Congress in Bologna.

1911: The crisis in the Theosophical Society deepens. In January, 'The Order of the Rising Sun,' which will soon become 'The Order of the Star in the East,' is founded for the coming world teacher, Krishnamurti. At the same time, Marie von Sivers, Rudolf Steiner's co-worker, falls ill. Fewer lectures are given, but important new ground is broken. In Prague, in March, Steiner meets Franz Kafka (1883–1924) and Hugo Bergmann (1883-1975). In April, he delivers his paper to the Philosophical Congress. He writes the second mystery drama, *The Soul's Probation* (CW 14). Also, while Marie von Sivers is convalescing, Rudolf Steiner begins work on *Calendar 1912/1913*, which will contain the 'Calendar of the Soul' meditations. On March 19, Anna (Eunike) Steiner dies. In September, Rudolf Steiner visits Einsiedeln, birthplace of Paracelsus. In December, Friedrich Rittelmeyer, future founder of the Christian Community, meets Rudolf Steiner. The *Johannes-Bauverein*, the 'building committee,' which would lead to the first Goetheanum (first planned for Munich), is also founded, and a preliminary committee for the founding of an independent association is created that, in the following year, will become the Anthroposophical Society. Important lecture cycles include *Occult Physiology* (CW 128); *Wonders of the World* (CW 129); *From Jesus to Christ* (CW 131). Other themes: esoteric Christianity; Christian Rosenkreutz; the spiritual guidance of humanity; the sense world and the world of the spirit.

1912: Despite the ongoing, now increasing crisis in the Theosophical Society, much is accomplished: *Calendar 1912/1913* is published; eurythmy is created; both the third mystery drama, *The Guardian of the Threshold* (CW 14) and *A Way of Self-Knowledge* (CW 16) are written. New (or renewed) themes included life between death and rebirth and karma and reincarnation. Other lecture cycles: *Spiritual Beings in the Heavenly Bodies and in the Kingdoms of Nature* (CW 136); *The Human Being in the Light of Occultism, Theosophy, and Philosophy* (CW 137); *The Gospel of St. Mark* (CW 139); and *The Bhagavad Gita and the Epistles of Paul* (CW 142). On May 8, Rudolf Steiner celebrates White Lotus Day, H.P. Blavatsky's death day, which he had faithfully observed for the past decade, for the last time. In August, Rudolf Steiner suggests the 'independent association' be called the 'Anthroposophical Society.' In September, the first eurythmy course takes place. In October, Rudolf Steiner declines recognition of a Theosophical Society lodge dedicated to the Star of the East and decides to expel all Theosophical Society members belonging to the order. Also, with Marie von Sivers, he first visits Dornach, near Basel, Switzerland, and they stand on the hill where the Goetheanum will be built. In November, a Theosophical Society lodge is opened by direct mandate from Adyar (Annie Besant). In December, a meeting of the German section occurs at which it is decided that belonging to the Order of the Star of the East is incompatible with membership in the Theosophical Society. December 28: informal founding of the Anthroposophical Society in Berlin.

1913: Expulsion of the German section from the Theosophical Society. February 2–3: Foundation meeting of the Anthroposophical Society. Board members include: Marie von Sivers, Michael Bauer, and Carl Unger. September 20: Laying of the foundation stone for the *Johannes Bau* (Goetheanum) in Dornach. Building begins immediately. The third mystery drama, *The Soul's Awakening* (CW 14), is completed. Also: *The Threshold of the Spiritual World* (CW 147). Lecture cycles include: *The Bhagavad Gita and the Epistles of Paul* and *The Esoteric Meaning of the Bhagavad Gita* (CW 146), which the Russian philosopher Nikolai Berdyaev attends; *The Mysteries of the East and of Christianity* (CW 144); *The Effects of Esoteric Development* (CW 145); and *The Fifth Gospel* (CW 148). In May, Rudolf Steiner is in London and Paris, where anthroposophical work continues.

1914: Building continues on the *Johannes Bau* (Goetheanum) in Dornach, with artists and co-workers from seventeen nations. The general assembly of the Anthroposophical Society takes place. In May, Rudolf Steiner visits Paris, as well as Chartres Cathedral. June 28: assassination in Sarajevo ('Now the catastrophe has happened!'). August 1: War is declared. Rudolf Steiner returns to Germany from Dornach—he will travel back and forth. He writes the last chapter of *The Riddles of Philosophy*. Lecture cycles include: *Human and Cosmic Thought* (CW 151); *Inner Being of Humanity between Death and a New Birth* (CW 153); *Occult Reading and Occult Hearing* (CW 156). December 24: marriage of Rudolf Steiner and Marie von Sivers.

1915: Building continues. Life after death becomes a major theme, also art. Writes: *Thoughts during a Time of War* (CW 24). Lectures include: *The Secret of Death* (CW 159); *The Uniting of Humanity through the Christ Impulse* (CW 165).

1916: Rudolf Steiner begins work with Edith Maryon (1872–1924) on the sculpture 'The Representative of Humanity' ('The Group'—Christ, Lucifer, and Ahriman). He also works with the alchemist Alexander von Bernus on the quarterly *Das Reich*. He writes *The Riddle of Humanity* (CW 20). Lectures include: *Necessity and Freedom in World History and Human Action* (CW 166); *Past and Present in the Human Spirit* (CW 167); *The Karma of Vocation* (CW 172); *The Karma of Untruthfulness* (CW 173).

1917: Russian Revolution. The U.S. enters the war. Building continues. Rudolf Steiner delineates the idea of the 'threefold nature of the human being' (in a public lecture March 15) and the 'threefold nature of the social organism' (hammered out in May-June with the help of Otto von Lerchenfeld and Ludwig Polzer-Hoditz in the form of two documents titled *Memoranda*, which were distributed in high places). August–September: Rudolf Steiner writes *The Riddles of the Soul* (CW 20). Also: commentary on 'The Chymical Wedding of Christian Rosenkreutz' for Alexander Bernus (*Das Reich*). Lectures include: *The Karma of Materialism* (CW 176); *The Spiritual Background of the Outer World: The Fall of the Spirits of Darkness* (CW 177).

1918: March 18: peace treaty of Brest-Litovsk—'Now everything will truly enter chaos! What is needed is cultural renewal.' June: Rudolf Steiner visits Karlstein (Grail) Castle outside Prague. Lecture cycle: *From Symptom to Reality in Modern History* (CW 185). In mid-November, Emil Molt, of the Waldorf-Astoria Cigarette Company, has the idea of founding a school for his workers' children.

1919: Focus on the threefold social organism: tireless travel, countless lectures, meetings, and publications. At the same time, a new public stage of Anthroposophy emerges as cultural renewal begins. The coming years will see initiatives in pedagogy, medicine, pharmacology, and agriculture. January 27: threefold meeting: ' We must first of all, with the money we have, found free schools that can bring people what they need.' February: first public eurythmy performance in Zurich. Also: 'Appeal to the German People' (CW 24), circulated March 6 as a newspaper insert. In April, *Towards Social Renewal* (CW 23) appears—'perhaps the most widely read of all books on politics appearing since the war.' Rudolf Steiner is asked to undertake the 'direction and leadership' of the school founded by the Waldorf-Astoria Company. Rudolf Steiner begins to talk about the 'renewal' of education. May 30: a building is selected and purchased for the future Waldorf School. August–September, Rudolf Steiner gives a lecture course for Waldorf teachers, *The Foundations of Human Experience (Study of Man)* (CW 293). September 7: Opening of the first Waldorf School. December (into January): first science course, the *Light Course* (CW 320).

1920: The Waldorf School flourishes. New threefold initiatives. Founding of limited companies *Der Kommende Tag* and *Futurum A.G.* to infuse spiritual values into the economic realm. Rudolf Steiner also focuses on the sciences. Lectures: *Introducing Anthroposophical Medicine* (CW 312); *The Warmth Course* (CW 321); *The Boundaries of Natural Science* (CW 322); *The Redemption of Thinking* (CW 74). February: Johannes Werner

Klein—later a co-founder of the Christian Community—asks Rudolf Steiner about the possibility of a 'religious renewal,' a 'Johannine church.' In March, Rudolf Steiner gives the first course for doctors and medical students. In April, a divinity student asks Rudolf Steiner a second time about the possibility of religious renewal. September 27–October 16: anthroposophical 'university course.' December: lectures titled *The Search for the New Isis* (CW 202).

1921: Rudolf Steiner continues his intensive work on cultural renewal, including the uphill battle for the threefold social order. 'University' arts, scientific, theological, and medical courses include: *The Astronomy Course* (CW 323); *Observation, Mathematics, and Scientific Experiment* (CW 324); the *Second Medical Course* (CW 313); *Colour*. In June and September-October, Rudolf Steiner also gives the first two 'priests' courses' (CW 342 and 343). The 'youth movement' gains momentum. Magazines are founded: *Die Drei* (January), and—under the editorship of Albert Steffen (1884–1963)—the weekly, *Das Goetheanum* (August). In February–March, Rudolf Steiner takes his first trip outside Germany since the war (Holland). On April 7, Steiner receives a letter regarding 'religious renewal,' and May 22–23, he agrees to address the question in a practical way. In June, the Klinical-Therapeutic Institute opens in Arlesheim under the direction of Dr. Ita Wegman. In August, the Chemical-Pharmaceutical Laboratory opens in Arlesheim (Oskar Schmiedel and Ita Wegman are directors). The Clinical Therapeutic Institute is inaugurated in Stuttgart (Dr. Ludwig Noll is director); also the Research Laboratory in Dornach (Ehrenfried Pfeiffer and Günther Wachsmuth are directors). In November–December, Rudolf Steiner visits Norway.

1922: The first half of the year involves very active public lecturing (thousands attend); in the second half, Rudolf Steiner begins to withdraw and turn toward the Society—'The Society is asleep.' It is 'too weak' to do what is asked of it. The businesses—*Der Kommende Tag* and *Futurum A.G.*—fail. In January, with the help of an agent, Steiner undertakes a twelve-city German lecture tour, accompanied by eurythmy performances. In two weeks he speaks to more than 2,000 people. In April, he gives a 'university course' in The Hague. He also visits England. In June, he is in Vienna for the East–West Congress. In August–September, he is back in England for the Oxford Conference on Education. Returning to Dornach, he gives the lectures *Philosophy, Cosmology, and Religion* (CW 215), and gives the third priests' course (CW 344). On September 16, The Christian Community is founded. In October–November, Steiner is in Holland and England. He also speaks to the youth: *The Youth Course* (CW 217). In December, Steiner gives lectures titled *The Origins of Natural Science* (CW 326), and *Humanity and the World of Stars: The Spiritual Communion of Humanity* (CW 219). December 31: Fire at the Goetheanum, which is destroyed.

1923: Despite the fire, Rudolf Steiner continues his work unabated. A very hard year. Internal dispersion, dissension, and apathy abound. There is conflict—between old and new visions—within the Society. A wake-up call is needed, and Rudolf Steiner responds with renewed lecturing vitality. His focus: the spiritual context of human life; initiation science; the course of the year; and community building. As a foundation for an artistic school, he creates a series of pastel sketches. Lecture cycles: *The Anthroposophical Movement; Initiation Science* (CW 227) (in England at the Penmaenmawr Summer School); *The Four Seasons and the Archangels* (CW 229); *Harmony of the Creative Word* (CW 230); *The Supersensible Human* (CW 231), given in Holland for the founding of the Dutch society. On November 10, in response to the failed Hitler-Ludendorff putsch in Munich, Steiner closes his Berlin residence and moves the *Philosophisch-Anthroposophisch Verlag* (Press) to Dornach. On December 9, Steiner begins the serialization of his *Autobiography: The Course of My Life* (CW 28) in *Das Goetheanum*. It will continue to appear weekly, without a break, until his death. Late December–early January: Rudolf Steiner re-founds the Anthroposophical Society (about 12,000 members internationally) and takes over its leadership. The new board members are: Marie Steiner, Ita Wegman, Albert Steffen, Elisabeth Vreede, and Günther Wachsmuth. (See *The Christmas Meeting for the Founding of the General Anthroposophical Society*, CW 260). Accompanying lectures: *Mystery Knowledge and Mystery Centres* (CW 232); *World History in the Light of Anthroposophy* (CW 233). December 25: the Foundation Stone is laid (in the hearts of members) in the form of the 'Foundation Stone Meditation.'

1924: January 1: having founded the Anthroposophical Society and taken over its leadership, Rudolf Steiner has the task of 'reforming' it. The process begins with a weekly newssheet ('What's Happening in the Anthroposophical Society') in which Rudolf Steiner's 'Letters to Members' and 'Anthroposophical Leading Thoughts' appear (CW 26). The next step is the creation of a new esoteric class, the 'first class' of the 'University of Spiritual Science' (which was to have been followed, had Rudolf Steiner lived longer, by two more advanced classes). Then comes a new language for Anthroposophy—practical, phenomenological, and direct; and Rudolf Steiner creates the model for the second Goetheanum. He begins the series of extensive 'karma' lectures (CW 235–40); and finally, responding to needs, he creates two new initiatives: biodynamic agriculture and curative education. After the middle of the year, rumours begin to circulate regarding Steiner's health. Lectures: January–February, *Anthroposophy* (CW 234); February: *Tone Eurythmy* (CW 278); June: *The Agriculture Course* (CW 327); June–July: *Speech Eurythmy* (CW 279); *Curative Education* (CW 317); August: (England, 'Second International Summer School'), *Initiation Consciousness: True and False Paths in Spiritual Investigation* (CW 243); September: *Pastoral Medicine* (CW 318). On September 26, for the first time, Rudolf Steiner cancels a lecture. On September 28, he gives his last lecture. On September 29, he withdraws to his studio in the carpenter's shop; now he is definitively ill. Cared for by Ita Wegman, he continues working, however, and writing the weekly installments of his *Autobiography* and *Letters to the Members/Leading Thoughts* (CW 26).

1925: Rudolf Steiner, while continuing to work, continues to weaken. He finishes *Extending Practical Medicine* (CW 27) with Ita Wegman.
On March 30, around ten in the morning, Rudolf Steiner dies

INDEX

A NOTE FROM RUDOLF STEINER PRESS

We are an independent publisher and registered charity (non-profit organisation) dedicated to making available the work of Rudolf Steiner in English translation. We care a great deal about the content of our books and have hundreds of titles available – as printed books, ebooks and in audio formats.

As a publisher devoted to anthroposophy…

- We continually commission translations of previously unpublished works by Rudolf Steiner and invest in re-translating, editing and improving our editions.
- We are committed to making anthroposophy available to all by publishing introductory books as well as contemporary research.
- Our new print editions and ebooks are carefully checked and proofread for accuracy, and converted into all formats for all platforms.
- Our translations are officially authorised by Rudolf Steiner's estate in Dornach, Switzerland, to whom we pay royalties on sales, thus assisting their critical work.

So, look out for Rudolf Steiner Press as a mark of quality and support us today by buying our books, or contact us should you wish to sponsor specific titles or to support the charity with a gift or legacy.